HOW TO BE
HAPPY
IN AN
UNHAPPY
WORLD

D0067074

Books by Marie Chapian

CHRISTIAN LIVING

Telling Yourself the Truth,
with William Backus—ECPA Gold
Book Award

*Why Do I Do What I Don't Want
to Do?* with William Backus

Love and Be Loved

Mothers and Daughters

Growing Closer

*Close Friends: Making Them,
Keeping Them*

Staying Happy in an Unhappy World

The Confident, Dynamic Woman

Angels in Our Lives

God in the Mirror,
with Miles McPherson

BIOGRAPHIES

The Emancipation of Robert Sadler,
with Robert Sadler

Help Me Remember, Help Me Forget

In the Morning of My Life,
with Tom Netherton

*Of Whom the World Was
Not Worthy*

Escape from Rage

Forgive Me, with Cathy Crowell
Webb—Cornerstone Book
of the Year

Back on Course,
with Gavin MacLeod

The Other Side of Suffering,
with John Ramsey

HEALTH AND FITNESS

Fun to Be Fit

Free to Be Thin, with Neva Coyle

The All-New Free to Be Thin,
with Neva Coyle

Slimming Down and Growing Up,
with Neva Coyle

DEVOTIONALS

His Thoughts toward Me

His Gifts toward Me

Discovering Joy

Making His Heart Glad

The Secret Place of Strength

God's Heart for You

Talk to Me, Jesus: The Journal

*Talk to Me, Jesus:
365-Day Devotional*

*Walk with Me, Jesus:
365-Day Devotional*

*Am I the Only One Here with Faded
Genes?* (teen devotional)—Gold
Medallion Award

Feeling Small, Walking Tall
(teen devotional)

CHILDREN'S BOOKS

Mustard Seed Library for Children

Alula-Belle Blows into Town

Alula-Belle Saves Ice Cream Beach

*Harold and I, an Incredible Journey
Consisting of Supernatural Events*
(illustrated by author)

POETRY

City Psalms

Mind Things

Slow Dance on Stilts—San Diego
First Place Book Award

HOW TO BE
HAPPY
IN AN
UNHAPPY
WORLD

Marie Chapian

Revell

a division of Baker Publishing Group
Grand Rapids, Michigan

Published by Revell
a division of Baker Publishing Group
P.O. Box 6287, Grand Rapids, MI 49516-6287
www.revellbooks.com

Printed in the United States of America

Library of Congress Cataloging-in-Publication Data
Chapian, Marie.
   How to be happy in an unhappy world / Marie Chapian.
      pages cm
   Includes bibliographical references.
   ISBN 978-0-8007-2631-7 (pbk.)
   1. Happiness—Religious aspects—Christianity. I. Title.
BV4647.J68C425 2015
248.4—dc23   2015024817

Author is represented by the literary agency of Alive Communications, Inc., 7680 Goddard St., Suite 200, Colorado Springs, CO 80920, www.alivecommunications.com.

In keeping with biblical principles of creation stewardship, Baker Publishing Group advocates the responsible use of our natural resources. As a member of the Green Press Initiative, our company uses recycled paper when possible. The text paper of this book is composed in part of post-consumer waste.

15   16   17   18   19   20   21   7   6   5   4   3   2   1

green
press
INITIATIVE

Contents

You can pursue happiness,
or you can create it.

Introduction

God didn't create us powerless over our mental and emotional states, and He doesn't abandon us like sitting ducks when life and the world take their relentless potshots at us. He gives us the perfect tools we need to attain lasting happiness—tools that have been here all along. In this book, we'll journey into the regions of our souls to discover within us what needs discovering and how to use the magnificent tools God gives us to live happy lives.

Happiness isn't merely the absence of unhappiness, nor is it exactly the opposite of unhappiness. It's neither euphoria nor rapturous joy because those are not enduring emotions. They come and go. You receive a gift and you're thrilled, you're elated. Six months later, chances are you've forgotten the moment entirely.

I like challenge and hard work, but when it comes to working for happiness, that's way too exhausting. Working for happiness is like hauling bricks. It wears you out. Fast. And when you have to labor for happiness, it comes across as shallow and empty. There you are, making your lists and working hard at doing what you think will make you happy, but because of its fickle nature, happiness continually slips through the cracks of your good intentions and resolutions. Happiness isn't something we earn or manufacture; it's something *we already possess inside*. We just need to learn the skills to corral it. That's what this book is about.

When I decided I was going to learn about this thing called happiness, I made a decision to combat depression and heartbreak and to embark on an all-out personal happiness journey. At the time, such an adventure seemed daunting to me, crazy even, but I knew that good things were ahead if I could just figure out *how* to reach out and take them.

I moved forward on my journey with happiness as the pot of gold at the end of the rainbow. What was happiness? I had seen a quotation by G. B. Shaw taped on a friend's computer that went something like this: "If you stay busy doing the things you like to do, you won't have time to be concerned about whether you are happy or not." That sounded quite clever until I really thought about it. These were more like the words of a person with a broken heart: "I'll just stay busy so I don't have to deal with my pain."

Avoiding pain creates more pain. I tried it, and it didn't work. I couldn't escape pain. Heartbreak, sorrow, grief, and loneliness are unavoidable in life, and when I crunched these feelings under a steamroller of busyness and hard work, I only increased the pain.

The questions I asked were, "How do I hold on to happiness and not lose it? Are there keys to staying happy in an unhappy world?"

I found that most people are resigned to believe that if they aren't unhappy, they must be happy. That kind of thinking is on the order of, "If I'm not sick, I must be well."

Functional depression can be like living with mice in the ceiling. You hear the mice, but you ignore the scratching and clatter of feet overhead. You're unhappy in your bones, but you carry on with a smile and ignore the messages you're giving yourself. I had yet to learn that happiness is a skill we teach ourselves, and when I finally came to that brilliant conclusion, my life took off like a bullet in the wind.

I believe God's intention for His children is to know happiness that's not fleeting or temporary but something that can be permanently lodged inside. I wrote a book called *Staying Happy in an Unhappy World* back in 1985, and the book's success told me I wasn't alone in my search and my desire for more than momentary feel-good answers. We've come a long way since then, but this new book takes its inspiration from that first journey into attaining and *holding on to* happiness.

I researched various contemporary and ancient programs on human well-being and happiness and found that most focus on the sense of contentment and happiness with life as it is in the *present*. The Bible agrees with this concept, of course. "*This* is the day the LORD has made. We will rejoice and be glad in it" (Ps. 118:24, emphasis added).

The avenues of Eastern religion, along with New Age philosophy, tell us that every human being has a capacity for happiness, so once we set our mind to be happy, our determination will help us fulfill that vision. But here's where the Bible disagrees and tells us we need more than *self*-determination. Buddha and Solomon do concur on one point, and that is the impermanence of this life. Solomon wrote in the book of Ecclesiastes that all is vanity, fleeting, and transitory; there's nothing permanent on the earth. Solomon also wrote, however, "I know that whatever God does, it shall be forever" (3:14).

Is it possible to be happy and *stay* happy? I learned that without happiness *skills*, the answer is no. We'll sink, like Peter trying to walk on water. Peter wasn't spiritually fit to pull off such a feat because he needed more spiritual training. Same with us. We need to be trained by God, not the world. All the positive affirmations in the world couldn't have kept Peter above water.

I'm surprised at the attitude of some people that happiness is something that happens randomly, like luck. Happiness doesn't just drop on us from the sky, like manna in the wilderness. *Happiness is a skill you teach yourself.*

As I made my happiness journey, I conducted surveys to record my findings, and this one in particular was eye-opening. I interviewed men and women from all walks of life, ages twenty-five to seventy-five, and asked them to focus on a certain random period in their adult life and to tell me if they were happy or not during that period. Considering there were no highs or lows during that particular time, such as births, weddings, deaths, divorces, sickness, college finals, lottery wins, etc., did they think of it as a happy time or not? They were to identify the period of time as happy or unhappy on a scale of 1 to 5:

1 = unhappy; 2 = mostly unhappy; 3 = neutral; 4 = mostly happy; 5 = very happy.

It was extremely difficult for the people I surveyed to answer truthfully how they felt. Eighty-five percent responded "very happy." Later, after a short time lapse, they were given another set of questions. When these same people were asked to name the five happiest periods in their lives, not one of them named the one on the survey they had marked "very happy."

Neuroscience research is now telling us we can change the way our brains are shaped by how we think. In the beginning, God created our brains as tools to anticipate and overcome dangers, to be on the alert for danger. The human nervous system scans for, reacts to, stores, and recalls negative information, and the natural result is a residue of stored negativity, thus shaping the brain and creating a desperate need for God to *renew* our brain, bestow on us "the mind of Christ" (1 Cor. 2:16), so we can say, "I am a new brain creature in Christ. Behold, all things have become new!" (see 2 Cor. 5:17).

Isn't it comforting to know that when we go to sleep at night, God's overarching blessing is upon our neurons, hypothalamus, amygdala, explicit and implicit memories? We can't escape loss and hurt. They are part of the fabric of life. But there's absolutely nothing in our DNA that says we can't tolerate and even thrive during disaster and heartbreak. I always tell my clients and students that when we get our hearts broken, we don't break in half; rather, we *chip*.

As I look back on my life, I see how hard I worked to be what I thought God wanted me to be, and maybe you're a bit like me on this. We can live our lives thinking we're okay when we aren't. Psalm 144:15 says, "*Happy* are the people whose God is the LORD" (emphasis added). I came to the realization that serving God in itself doesn't necessarily make us happy, and that's when I woke up and began to search for and practice the happiness skills I'm sharing with you in this book.

Unhappiness can be an asset when it pushes us to wake up and stop avoiding our emotional injuries and sufferings no matter how painful they may be and face them. If you're like every other human on the planet, you've probably got what we call "misbeliefs" influencing your daily life. These misbeliefs are like nasty bug bites, and they don't go away on their own.

Misbelief is a term coined by Dr. William Backus for the continual lies we tell ourselves. They're evident in our inner dialogue, our self-talk, and they aren't true. "Misbeliefs generally *appear as truth* to the person repeating them to himself . . . partly because the sufferer has never examined or questioned these erroneous assumptions. . . . If you tell yourself untruths or lies, you will *believe untruths and lies*. If you believe something, you'll act on it."[1]

Here are some examples.

"I failed once; I'll probably fail again."

"I'm smart and talented, and therefore I should have more privileges than others."

"Nobody will ever love me."

Steven Pressfield gives a reason for these lies that he calls "resistance." He says, "Resistance is experienced as fear; the degree of fear equates the strength of resistance, and therefore, the more fear we feel about a specific enterprise, the more certain we can be that that enterprise is important to us and to the growth of our soul."[2]

Misbeliefs cause us to deny ourselves pleasure and every good thing God offers us, and throughout this book, we'll examine our self-talk to see where misbeliefs are robbing us of the flourishing lives we were ordained to live.

I suggest you create a happiness journal to keep notes as you go through the exercises in this book. This is an exciting process and a welcome addition to the benefits of self-discovery. You'll find your happiness journal to be an important part of your journey both now and later. (I like to use regular paper notebooks for my journal, but you may prefer your tablet, cell phone, laptop, or iPad. Whatever works best for you.) You'll have fun with some new brain exercises and learn the art of stillness and focusing through what I call Quiet Prayer. With its roots in ancient Christianity, this form of prayer is, for most of us today, quite new and revolutionary. I introduce Quiet Prayer to get you started on an inner journey that's different from the ordinary prayer we're accustomed to. True and lasting happiness remains elusive without inner peace, and the Quiet Prayer moments you'll experience here are to help release within you a sense of peace to know deeper intimacy with God. A truly happy heart is a peaceful heart, and for most of us, this takes practice.

I share honestly and openly with you what I've learned through my own swim upriver as well as through my work as counselor, certified life coach, spiritual director, minister, author, and teacher. I'll be talking about many people to illustrate different aspects of happiness, so maybe you'll relate to some of them. They're real people with identities changed, of course.

When your negative, miserable past calls you, don't answer. It has nothing new to say. Dare to be happy. I believe God is calling you to a higher life, no longer white-knuckling it with exhausting determination and long lists of feel-good must-dos. Our God wants to surprise you with more love in your life and more happiness than you thought possible. It happened to me. Really.

He wants our hearts and minds to be one with His. That's why I'm convinced that we can each become happy and stay happy in an unhappy world.

Do it for you,
          for God,
                    for the world.

Good-bye to the Victim

When I was five years old, my mother picked me up from kindergarten one day and took me to visit my grandmother. I was named after her, and I adored her. She was fragile and elegant and educated. I don't remember her ever being well. My one enduring memory of her is seeing her sitting up in bed with her hair combed in a neat, soft pile on top of her head, her long, thin arms at her sides. She used to read to me by the hour from her wonderful and brilliantly illustrated storybooks. Her voice was clear and light, and I loved her funny-shaped hands, her sparkling green eyes. She had a sweet smile, and no matter when I popped into her room, she was happy to see me.

We lived next door to my grandparents, and I spent more time with her than I did at home. On the day when my mother picked me up from kindergarten, I ran into my grandmother's bedroom while my mother prepared lunch. I was alone when I found her lying glassy-eyed, staring at the wall. Her breakfast dishes were on the floor, and there was cereal splattered on the wall. She was talking to me, her tongue thick and her voice so soft that I had to put my face next to hers to hear her. Her hands clutched mine, cold, thin, the life draining from them. When my mother found me, I was snuggled beside my grandma in the bed, thinking she was asleep. My mother had to coax me to stop combing her hair and singing to her. She was dead.

Years later, I understood the emotional impact my grandma's death had on our family. My mother had insisted our families live in an apartment building next door to each other so she could nurse her mother back to health. She believed she could restore her to her former healthy and vibrant self. When my grandmother died, my mother was shattered. She was the oldest of seven children and had felt responsible. Her reaction to her mother's death was a mixture of grief and guilt. She just couldn't believe her mother had died. She told me years later how she believed she was a complete failure in caring for her mother because she couldn't keep her alive. The first phase of grief, "I can't believe it," can take several months to go through, even longer. At this point in her life, my mother could see no escape from her pain. Feelings of loss and defeat immobilized her.

A lovely couple I once knew had an outwardly happy life until the husband's father was killed in a freak airplane crash. This once-happy couple was suddenly thrown into a morass of confusion and sorrow. The father had been a major character in their marriage. Without him, depression and sadness permeated their lives. In time, this couple separated. Without the husband's father's powerful influence, their foundation crumbled.

Another couple are parents of an only child, a teenager, who has turned his back on church and his parents' expectations of him. The parents see his behavior as mutiny. The wife tearfully told me, "I don't understand why this is happening to us. We're good people. Why couldn't our son be a good person?" Their son is not a bad person. Creative, yes—bad, no. He's trying out his wings, but moving in directions the parents don't understand or approve of doesn't make him a mutineer.

Victim misbeliefs include, "Things should always be the way I think they should be." And that is always followed by, "When things don't go as I think they should, it's absolutely terrible, awful, bad, unthinkable, disastrous." A victim way of thinking is, "I should be rewarded for my hard work and sacrifice," and it's this kind of thinking that erodes the heart's pure love. When things don't work out as hoped for, the victim [mis]believes, "I must accept misery and disappointment as a way of life."

A Victim or a Survivor

Suffering can make either survivors or victims out of us. My mother, in time, I'm happy to say, became a survivor. She experienced the emotional numbness of losing her mother, plus the feelings of defeat and guilt. She grieved, but as time wore on, she realized her need to let go. She thought maybe she wasn't a failure after all, and even if she was, did it disavow her value? Eventually, she chose to be a survivor, not a victim. She chose to find a better solution than self-denigration. All of this I learned much later when I was an adult as she shared the pain of her guilt and sorrow with me. I learned much from her powerful emotional achievement. She felt she had let down her mother, her family, and God too, but she rose to a higher level of love and grace when she stopped being a victim. Only then could she tap into the lasting gifts of happiness.

Do you know the difference between a victim and a survivor? The times you're depressed and unhappy in your life may be due to victim consciousness, victim thinking, and victim behavior. Nobody has to stay a victim. We can be survivors. Here are some differences between the two.

17

The Victim	The Survivor
Thinks because bad things have happened before, they will always happen.	Tells themselves that when bad things happen, it is not the end of the world.
Thinks, "Everything happens to me."	Knows and experiences trouble and pain but doesn't lose sight of blessings.
Sees no way out of problems.	In suffering and trial says, "I can do all things through Christ who strengthens me."
Expects loss and failure to happen to them.	Is at peace with loss and failure without blame, guilt, or shame.
Is dependent on others for their well-being.	Creates a life without the belief that others are responsible for their well-being.
Feels rejected and left out.	Examines feelings of rejection to see if they're real, making positive and realistic changes to have and maintain rewarding and lasting relationships.
Takes no responsibility for their life.	Takes full responsibility for attitude, beliefs, feelings, and actions. This is true maturity.

The couple who lost the husband's father could not be called survivors. To this day, they believe the world is filled with evil and tragedy, and these beliefs are what shape the quality of their lives. Happiness eludes them because of their negative expectations of life. Victims feel the world is a dangerous place.

You can see why a victim is a person who lives in a constant state of fatigue or frustration. Life and relationships fail to produce rewards that the victim craves. A victim typically enters a relationship with another person hoping to fill a void in themselves. The object of affection can quickly become the center of their existence. Neurotic dependency is then followed by resentment for the very one the victim needs. Dependence becomes obsessional, and the results can be disastrous.

Dependent thinking is victim thinking, and when a person depends on someone else for their well-being, they can eventually despise that person.

Another form of victim behavior is the one most often mistaken for humility. The victim behaves humbly and is subservient and even selfless. But this is not self-denial. This is not humility. This is inordinately self-centered behavior. The victim is a self-indulgent person with numero uno always at the forefront. The victim with a mind-set based on "poor me" puts themselves down hoping for attention and a caring response.

This victim will bend over backwards to help some cause or person. One day when there is no payback or if they're not recognized for their appearance of selflessness, they'll lash out over how used and abused they are. When good deeds promote self-absorption, the good deeds turn sour.

Overcoming Victim Thinking

Is there a way out of victim thinking? Yes. If you recognize yourself in some of these victim descriptions, make note of them. Write them down to jar your awareness.

We can be deceived by our own emotions and ignorance. We tell ourselves our problems are due to others or the environment. We don't believe we're responsible for our own happiness. Our troubles are because others have used, abused, hurt, wounded, cheated, and stolen from us. You see, dear uncaring world, you've done this to me, and I have every right to be miserable!

But eventually we have to wake up. Though things may be unpleasant or downright bad, things are also good. Blessings do exist. You can't be victimized twenty-four hours a day every day of your life without even one glimmer of relief and respite. Nobody is a victim *all* the time. You can be hurt by others, mistreated, cheated, betrayed, and downright abused, but if you look truthfully at yourself, you'll see you've also been blessed. Many times in your life, you've been loved and admired and you've been pleased with yourself. See yourself in this light. It's the seed and flower of lasting happiness.

A real hero of mine is psychiatrist Viktor Frankl, who suffered horribly in a Nazi concentration camp in the Second World War. He told a fellow suffering prisoner as they painfully dug trenches in the hard earth, "This is where you've got to find your happiness—right here in this trench, in this camp." Dr. Frankl wrote later in *Man's Search for Meaning*, "What is to give light must endure burning." He went on, "Everything can be taken from a man but one thing: the last of human freedoms to choose one's attitude in any given set of circumstances, to choose one's own way."[1]

Happiness doesn't just fall on us from the sky. We choose it. It takes courage to be happy.

I've counseled couples who needed each other to blame their unhappiness on. They ignored the Bible's sweet advice, "Be kind to one another, tender-hearted, forgiving each other, just as God in Christ also has forgiven you" (Eph. 4:32 NASB). They were not courageous lovers but blame-putting, fault-finding foes. It takes courage to be forgiving. Unforgiveness keeps us bound to our pain.

Below are some statements that signal whether your victim thinking is hurting you and will only get worse if left unchecked. See if you can identify with any of them. Put a check by those that apply. If the statement only partially applies, still put a check beside it.

1. It's rarely my fault when things go wrong.
2. I'm beginning to feel increasingly cynical and critical about life in general.
3. I continually find fault with my co-workers for their mistakes and problems.

4. I put off doing what I know needs to be done until the last moment, or I don't do it at all.

5. I make excuses for not doing the work at hand because I (a) feel it's someone else's duty, or (b) don't want someone else to benefit or get the credit, or (c) just don't feel like doing it.

6. I'm disorganized at my job as well as at home.

7. I resent it when other people make more money, live better, and have more successful personal lives than I do.

8. I don't think there are many people in this world who are on my side.

9. I don't think anyone really understands me.

10. I'm afraid that when people get to know me, they won't like me.

11. I feel most people are competitive and not to be trusted.

If you checked four or more of the above statements, you're not in a happy place. Your life may be a mix of anxiety and needless pain. It could be that you feel constantly threatened by some impending doom or that the thought of living tomorrow with the troubles of today is overwhelming. Read on, because there is help.

A victim is not necessarily a crazy person racked with fits and mental agony, but they certainly display some neurotic behavior. A victim doesn't like the idea of change. A victim is likely to run away from challenges and deliberately appear weak to avoid unwanted responsibility. The weaker we are, the greater our dependency. The more dependent we are, the more self-absorbed we are. The dependent person is interested only in fulfilling themselves.

The Root of Unhappiness

Let's get at the root of our unhappiness. Positive or negative responses to events in life are directly related to the *meaning* we give them. In effect, we create our own neuroses. You're upset, say, because your husband just left the house without telling you where he was going. You feel angry and helpless. You want to go after him, pull his arm, and demand an explanation. "I can't handle it when you don't tell me where you're going," you despair.

Your despair is self-inflicted and has little to do with your husband's behavior. Your words "I can't handle it" more often than not mean "I won't." You're saying, "I won't do something positive and assertive to enrich this situation." Is it that you relish being weak and helpless? "I can't change anything for the better" really means I won't, and you think you have the right to feel angry.

Helplessness is:

- a desire to do something but not doing it
- not being certain you'll do something well, so avoiding it
- feeling betrayed when your child rejects your way of life instead of listening and showing compassion
- wanting to have a happy relationship with someone but refusing to give too much of yourself because they may decide to dump you, and rejection is the worst thing on earth

As we've seen, a victim feels dependent on other people and blames them for their problems and pain. A person can actually become so detached from themselves that they stop feeling they are the actual person living their life. This is schizoid alienation and a sign of our times. Uncertainty about life itself, and our very existence, is at the core of much unhappiness.

If we live as a victim, we are always in a state of longing. Never satisfied. We turn our frustrations and anger inward and suffer from insatiable and unidentified longings that nothing and nobody can fulfill. We mistake "need" for "cherish." We desperately *need* another person. We have a tendency to regard loved ones as "commodities." Relationships based on and dictated by personal

Mid-Continent Public Library

Checked Out Items 10/9/2021 17:02
XXXXXXXXXX0940

Item Title	Due Date
30004005857988	11/6/2021
Spiritual rebel : a positively addictive guide to finding deeper perspective & higher purpose	
30004006730242	11/6/2021
The book of awakening : having the life you want by being present to the life you have	
30004008584753	11/6/2021
Chakras, food, and you : tap your individual energy system for health, healing, and harmonious weight	
30003013942428	11/6/2021
When "spiritual but not religious" is not enough : seeing God in surprising places, even the church	
30003017044213	11/6/2021
How to be happy in an unhappy world	
30004004931990	11/6/2021
Haunted : malevolent ghosts, night terrors, and threatening phantoms	
30003018038602	11/6/2021
Natural meditation : refreshing your spirit through nature	

Amount Outstanding: $3.45

Discover how the Library can help kids, parents, teachers, and caregivers with all your back-to-school needs. Learn more at mymcpl.org/BackToSchool.

Checked Out Items 10/9/2021 17:02
XXXXXXXXXXXX0940

Item Title	Due Date
30004005857988	11/6/2021
Spiritual rebel : a positively addictive guide to finding deeper perspective & higher purpose	
30004005730242	11/6/2021
The book of awakening : having the life you want by being present to the life you have	
30004005584753	11/6/2021
Chakras, food, and you : tap your individual energy system for health, healing, and harmonious weight	
30003013942428	11/6/2021
When "spiritual but not religious" is not enough : seeing God in surprising places, even the church	
30003017044213	11/6/2021
How to be happy in an unhappy world	
30004004931990	11/6/2021
Haunted : malevolent ghosts, night terrors, and threatening phantoms	
30003018038602	11/6/2021
Natural meditation : refreshing your spirit through nature	

Amount Outstanding: $3.45

need culminate only in what Erich Fromm described as "fusion without integrity."[2]

The couple whose husband's father died represents fusion without integrity. When the father died and was no longer there as their bulwark, it was as though they themselves ceased to exist.

When we experience inner emptiness, we try desperately to fill the emptiness, and we can act out a child's sense of deprivation. The advertising industry incessantly feeds us promises of happiness that isn't happiness. We buy into fantasy that doesn't fulfill.

As part of my research for this book, I interviewed and observed people in many situations. One was what I called my Bus Project. I'd board local buses in various cities with my journal and write down everything I saw and heard. (Air travel is different because people tend to act differently on longer trips than on a local bus.) I wanted to know what made people happy, what they talked about, what they read, what they typically did as they sat in a place where they were neither here nor there between local destinations.

The people I observed on my many bus rides who appeared to be content were those who had a smile for a stranger, who gave up their seat for someone else, whose body language said they were alert and alive. The next time you're on a bus or a train, notice these things. Use the opportunity to take a good look at yourself.

The absence of problems doesn't make us happy. You don't need a vacation from your busy daily life. What you need is time with God in the *midst* of your busy daily life.

Replace the Bad with the Good

A quantum mechanical principle, the Pauli Exclusion Principle, states that no two particles can occupy the same space at the same time. Let's apply the principle to our lives. The book in your hand

and your coffee cup, for instance, can't occupy the same space. Your hat and your shoe can't occupy the same space. The space will hold one thing or the other, but not both. You can place your hat on top of your shoe and the cup on top of the book, but neither one can occupy the exact same area of space at the same time. Occupying space is what separates matter from light. Matter takes up a volume of space, and no other matter particle can occupy it.

Look at yourself. The peace in you can't occupy the same space as the anxiety in you. Happiness can't share the same space with fear. Love can't share the same space with bitterness. In order for love to operate fully within you, bitterness must step aside. In order for faith to manifest itself fully in you, doubt must fall away. Anxiety must move over for peace to reign in you. In the same way, if you hang on to negative emotions, they will muscle out the good ones.

If you've experienced painful events and gone through horribly hurtful situations, begin to use the methods I'm sharing in this book to push out the negative emotions. I've been there. I've clung to Joel 2:25 to help me see more clearly God's purpose, and you can do the same: "I will restore to you the years that the swarming locust has eaten, the crawling locust, the consuming locust, and the chewing locust." This is a promise we can stand on. God can restore to us what has been stolen from us and what has wounded us in our lives.

Here's a short, two-point exercise for something that happened in the past:

1. Identify the situation for what it was at the time. Remember exactly what happened. Take your time. Try not to be led by your emotions.
2. Leave the situation right where it is. Let go! Imagine you're scooping it up in a bag and tying a heavy rope around it. Tell the Lord, "Your burden is light and your yoke easy. Take

this from me. I don't want to think like a victim," and toss it away.

That may have been difficult to do, and if you're like me, you may have to come back to this exercise again. To be free deep inside, you must get rid of your victim mentality. Know that God is in the business of rebuilding, renewing, restoring, and blessing.

You can become so accustomed to a victim mentality that you think it's the real you. It's not the real you. Stop hauling it around with you! My mother had become dependent not on a person but on her heroic cause to make my grandmother well again. She had to come to grips with this loss and appraise herself as well as her loss. Years later, she would again be forced to face a trauma when my dad was killed in a train accident. She, as well as my brother, sister, and I, had to discover meaning through severe pain of loss. Our grief over his sudden death took over our lives. But my mother became a woman of deep faith and inner peace and a shining example to our entire family. I learned through observing her that peace is not the absence of suffering and loss. Peace is not the absence of strife or trials. Peace can be found in the worst suffering, cacophony, and hopeless situations. Peace can be found in the midst of pain and turmoil, and the discovery of this is the secret to not only a happier life but also a glorious life.

Take the opportunity to become the free person you were born to be. When you close yourself off from learning new happiness skills, you do so for two reasons: one, you inwardly believe your life will always be the way it is; and two, you believe life was meant to be unhappy and those of us who preach happiness are deluded. Both notions are untrue. They are misbeliefs.

Answer the following:

1. Is it difficult for you to face the thought that you may be wrong?
2. Do you think it's possible that God has a far better life for you and a wonderful future?

Then do the following and write your answers in your happiness journal:

1. Write, "I can't be an overcomer and a victim at the same time."
2. Write five ways you'll stop being a victim this week.

Though we live in a victim-bound world, refuse to be a victim. Pray these words:

Father, in the name of Jesus, I give up my role as victim.
I will not be victimized.
I will overcome.
I will love.
I will face my inadequacies.
I will dare to be imperfect because you are perfect, and it's your perfection I trust.
I will be grateful.
I will forgive.
I will choose to be happy, not tomorrow or next year but right now.

Bury these words deep into the depths of your soul: "We know that all things work together for good to those who love God, to those who are called according to His purpose!" (Rom. 8:28).

The Art of Quiet Prayer

Here's your first five-minute Quiet Prayer. Quieting your mind, pulling yourself into the now of the moment, is a foreign concept to most of us. We simply don't know how to still our minds. And ironically enough, it is the route to real happiness. I'm talking about the kind of happiness that comes from deep inside us, so deep, so pure, so vast that outside influences simply can't twist, alter, or strangle it.

I began practicing Quiet Prayer with no idea what it meant. I was alone in my writing studio one evening praying when suddenly I heard a voice from deep inside me. I knew it was the Lord Jesus. The sound warmed me from head to toe. He said simply and quietly, "Won't you come sit with Me awhile?"

Sit with Him awhile. *God* was asking *me* to sit with Him awhile? (Imagine answering, "Not now. I'm praying.") He didn't ask me to *do* something or *go* somewhere. He just wanted me to *sit* with Him for a while. I didn't quite know how to do it, so I rolled out my exercise mat and I sat. He said sit, so I sat. I didn't say anything or do anything. I just sat. I sat with Him awhile. And every day after that I sat with Him awhile on my mat. I get up in the morning and roll out my exercise mat and sit. I do what He said: I sit. I don't talk. I just sit.

This was all new to me, let me tell you. In all my years of experience in Bible school, seminary, and teaching and studying the Word, I'd never had a class in simply sitting. Of the thousands of prayer meetings I've taken part in, I couldn't name one in which nobody said anything.

I knew nothing about the practice of stillness in prayer or what the holy Christian saints and mystics practiced centuries ago in their cloistered cells and monasteries. I thought "meditation" was something people from Eastern religions did, not something evangelical Christians engaged in. I began to research the ancient Christian tradition of meditation and the desert mystics— St. John of the Cross, St. Teresa, Julian of Norwich, and many others. With no experience, I took courses with contemporary leaders of Orthodox and Catholic centering prayer, and I studied the books of Thomas Merton, Henri Nouwen, Thomas Keating, Richard Rohr, John Maines, Cynthia Bourgeault, and others. I entered the oblate program of a Benedictine monastery. I went to contemplative prayer retreats, and I poured myself into the

Scriptures. I read, I prayed, I entered—I sat with Him a very long while.

Based on the centering prayer of the ancients brought forth from their cloistered walls in the 1970s by Fr. Thomas Keating and the Trappist monks, Quiet Prayer, as I'm calling it, is like entering into the heart of God and taking a seat. You look at Him, and He looks at you. I like what St. Catherine of Genoa passionately exclaimed: "Jesus in your heart! In your mind! The will of God in all your actions! But above all, love, God's entire love!"[3] I like the word *entire*. It's a beautiful word and exceptionally powerful when placed before the word *love*. God's love is entire, perfect, whole, complete, full, total, all-inclusive, absolute. His love for us, and in us, is absolutely, totally perfect, fully and wholly entire, lacking nothing. His love is eternity in us. If we are to be free of the victim mentality, we must pull away from whatever keeps us occupied and focus on God alone.

For Quiet Prayer, we center on the reality of Psalm 91:1, which reads, "He [or she] who dwells in the secret place of the Most High shall abide under the shadow of the Almighty." Quiet Prayer is a time to enter the secret place of the Most High and just sit with Him. It's a place where there are no words but simply the experience of sitting still with God in His presence while saying nothing, asking nothing, and having no expectations or desires—except to sit with Him. We're being with Him, and in being with Him, He transforms us.

It's an amazing concept when you think about it because we're so accustomed to talking! There is a place for intercession, praise, and worship, of course, but Quiet Prayer is different. Here you are sitting in stillness in God's presence, and nothing else. It's a time to concentrate on and absorb God's presence. You can enter this intensely personal Quiet Prayer time before or after your regular time of prayer. You may want to read a verse of Scripture before your Quiet Prayer to help center you for stillness. I suggest you try just five minutes to begin with.

To start, seek out a quiet place with no distractions, including music. Sit in a comfortable, upright, alert position with your spine straight, shoulders back, head relaxed, and eyes lightly closed. Remain as still and comfortable in your body as possible. It might take a minute or two for you to still your mind and settle into yourself. Keep yourself alert. This is not a relaxation exercise. Your body is alert, not resting. Your spine is erect. If you are sitting in a chair, your legs are not crossed. Your feet are flat on the floor. If you are sitting on the floor with legs crossed, keep your knees lower than your waist. Your hands are at your sides or comfortably on your lap.

For this first Quiet Prayer, you'll practice breathing and quieting your mind. Begin by taking some nice, deep breaths. Breathe deeply and slowly with smooth, even breaths. Listen to the sound of your breath as it travels in and out like waves of the ocean.

As thoughts, ideas, and images enter your mind, gently observe and let them go as you bring your focus back to your breath. You're quieting your mind. You're sitting alone with God. You are with Him, and He is with you.

When five minutes are up, gently open your eyes and make a note of the experience in your happiness journal. Don't be too quick to rush away. Stay for a moment with your Lord, who loves you, and think about what you just experienced.

The Call to Happiness

We're programmed to buy into a barrel of beliefs about happiness and then judge our lives according to those beliefs. One such belief is that the future will be better than the present. Things will always be happier tomorrow. So we continue to cling to hopes that fail us. Or we're taught that health, autonomy, social involvement, fulfilling work, and the quality of our environment are the real sources of happiness. But are they? When I read the court cases of convicted killers and pedophiles, many of them could check yes on all the above. Does that mean they're happy? And plenty of studies have shown that people who live ugly, unjust, and pointless lives claim, nonetheless, to be happy and fulfilled.

Or somehow we have the notion that the more money we make, the happier we'll be, yet between 1970 and 1990, average incomes in the United States rose by 300 percent, but there was no corresponding increase in our average well-being. Statistics prove that happiness and well-being fail to increase in spite of growing incomes. We can live in bigger houses, drive better cars, and make enough money to pay all our bills on time and still be discontent. Giving a miserable person a raise in pay to make him happy is like giving a frog an operatic score to make him a tenor.

Part of the problem is how we define happiness. *Happiness is not just a feeling; it's a state of being.*

Below is a list of ten common occurrences that produce short-term feelings of happiness. We can all pretty much agree on these. We feel good when:

1. something happens outside our control that's good, pleasant, and welcoming
2. a threat is removed or a pain assuaged
3. things go as planned
4. we feel genuinely loved by another person
5. we achieve something difficult
6. we win an award or hoped-for gain
7. good luck happens like winning at gambling or the lottery
8. we feel appreciated
9. we have the sensation that we're doing better than an opponent
10. something turns out for good when we hadn't expected it

But is it happiness we feel or simply a good feeling? Each of these are fleeting sensations, not absolute states. You aren't going to feel as good next year at this time as you feel right now for getting your work done on time today. You see a tattered guy on the street begging for money and you feel a brief "there but for the grace of God" sensation, but tomorrow you'll have forgotten all about it.

It's important to feel appreciated, to do a job well, to feel good when things go as planned. Without moments of happiness, we'd be robots. But this book is about *lasting* happiness, the kind that remains even when we're not appreciated or when plans go belly-up.

We get angry with ourselves for not getting what we need to be happy, and we get angry at the world around us for not giving us what we need to be happy. The problem is that real happiness—lasting happiness—comes from *within*. If it doesn't, it's elusive and distant—out there in the fickle arms of fate.

A 2012 World Happiness Report stated that no validated method had been found to substantially improve *long-term* happiness in a meaningful way for most people. I'm talking about finding and keeping long-term happiness as a way of life.

We've been influenced by intellectual pessimists such as Arthur Schopenhauer who tell us that happiness is an illusion. In Schopenhauer's essay titled "On the Suffering of the World," he wrote, "Work, worry, toil and trouble are indeed the lot of almost all men their whole life long."[1] Sigmund Freud and Jean-Paul Sartre claimed that anguish is our human lot, and happiness isn't included in the plan of creation. Friedrich Nietzsche saw nihilism as the outcome of a search for meaning, and so God is dead. Ludwig Wittgenstein said, "I don't know why we are here, but I'm pretty sure that it is not in order to enjoy ourselves."[2] He purported that to live is to suffer. I imagine Nietzsche to have been a grumpy sort of guy even though he liked art, and I don't think Wittgenstein must have been much fun either.

A Life of Purpose

Aristotle called the good life, or "happiness," *eudaimonia*, which is to say a life in which a person flourishes or fulfills their full potential. In other words, *eudaimonia* is happiness *on purpose*. Happiness on purpose means our entire lives are governed by purpose. I'm not happy just because I want to be happy. I'm happy because my life warrants it. Happiness is a natural result, a by-product, of my life's choices and purpose.

Happiness pursued at the cost of goodness or purpose, and void of God, is not happiness but something else entirely. Eat, drink, and be merry is hardly living life on purpose, and purpose is a requisite for lasting happiness. A purposeless life is an empty life under any standard. It's vital we find our lifetime purpose, which is only revealed through God. Without God, there's no possibility of *lasting* happiness.

I use the words *purpose* and *vision* interchangeably. I teach a workshop on finding God's purpose for our lives, and it includes the birth of a vision. That vision is all-inclusive. It is what we stand for in this world; it's the meaning for being alive.

You find your vision by looking at what you're passionate about. What would you lay down your life for? If, for example, you answered, "I'd lay down my life for my family," then your life's vision includes family and family values. How far will you extend it? Where will this take you? What does it mean?

Life purpose and vision are not choices to make glibly. My course runs six weeks, and my students and clients produce real spiritual sweat as they work at finding who they are in God's plan. Discover your vision and find your true life—and true happiness.

Vision Exercise

Name one thing you'd lay down your life for. Make it practical and real (not something like a beautiful sunset or a Hershey bar with almonds). Write it as one sentence only. After you've written your one sentence, take time to think about how this opens up your vision and informs and leads to a life purpose. Life purposes can change, so give yourself time to think about this. Write what the sentence means to you and how you might live it out in your daily life and in the months to come.

After you've done this, try naming one more thing you'd lay down your life for and do the same exercise. Let yourself be really free. There are no limits.

That famous philosopher Anonymous once said that you are never given a vision without being given the ability to achieve it.

Anonymous also said, "If you can conceive it, you can achieve it." Do I agree? When God is showing us what He wants to accomplish through us, yes!

The vision you have for your life needs to come from the heart and mind of God. He delivers it to your heart and soul because He has already fulfilled it for you. Your job is to step into the work of fulfilling your purpose, to get on the path that is already laid out for you. He has gone before you. He doesn't guarantee you'll have no snares and snafus along the way, but He does guarantee His wisdom, guidance, and courage. After all, it's His vision too.

One of the how-to-be-happy-in-an-unhappy-world effects, something most hedonistic pessimists don't possess, is a light-heartedness. Discovering the secrets of lasting happiness is a result of learning the skills of going within yourself and connecting with God in a deep and permanent way—and this is gladdening!

When you live inside the deep, glorious well of happiness through Christ, you're just plain fun to be around. You're the kind of person everyone wants to be around, like Jesus. You're at peace with yourself and the world. People want to know you. I want to know you. I want to laugh with you, sing with you, pray with you, play Scrabble with you. I want to go bike riding with you, picnic with you, listen to Chopin nocturnes with you, and dance all night with you.

The Perfectionist

The perfectionist hates to think of themselves as average. The very idea of being an average person in an average world is offensive to the perfectionist. The thought of being ordinary makes the perfectionist nervous. Their idea of perfection is an outward one, related to *doing*, not *being*. They rob themselves of real happiness by their enslavement to achieving, and they can never achieve enough. People, including family, never make the mark in the perfectionist's eye. One perfectionist's thirteen-year-old son complained his dad was home *too much*.

Perfectionist behavior is often learned in childhood when the love received from parents is conditional. A client of mine shared how he could not remember a time in his life when he felt he had been a truly good boy in his mother's eyes or that he had met her approval. Even when he graduated from college summa cum laude, his mother was unimpressed. He explained to her that *summa cum laude* was Latin and meant with greatest honor, the highest academic distinction, and the comment his mother made was, "I never heard it in church."

As a successful businessman, my client struggled for years with perfectionist attitudes. Without knowing it, he had taken on himself the attitude and voice of his fault-finding mother, who died without ever telling him she was proud of him or that she loved him.

I become emotional at such cruelties parents inflict on their children due to their own selfish, pained lives. My client needed to silence the critical, unloving voice in order to see his way to freedom. His mother had been a church-going woman, and this is what confused my client and kept him at a distance from God. I suggested he attend a men's Christian retreat, and reluctantly he went. He was deeply moved by the experience of being with men who encouraged one another in their faith walk, and when he came back, he was ready to begin my class in Quiet Prayer as a way to be still before God and learn more of His compassion and loving-kindness.

Perfectionism is sometimes an alternative way of saying "obsessive-compulsive." The Diagnostic and Statistical Manual of Mental Disorders (DSM-5) describes the obsessive-compulsive personality as being excessively rigid, over-inhibited, over-conscientious, over-dutiful, and unable to relax easily.

A certain degree of obsessiveness is helpful to have when you need to be hardworking and conscientious. If you must meet a goal or a deadline, a healthy amount of obsessiveness is beneficial. The industrious, organized, and efficient person knows it's important to be dedicated to doing a good job. But if that person behaves over-conscientiously and over-dutifully, burnout is imminent.

The time in your life when it is not neurotic to be obsessive-compulsive is when you're a student. Medical students, seminary students, and other graduate students would not get through the demands of school without being committed to their work to a degree that is over and beyond the call of everyday living. When you're hard-pressed to accomplish a task, when you have a deadline at hand, when you are working on a project requiring more work than an ordinary job, and when you find that you must work many more hours a day than usual, you are not necessarily behaving neurotically. Nor should you accept labels such as "workaholic." There are some times in life when you must work harder and longer than people who don't have the same job or exam or deadline that's on your plate. A problem develops when such behavior becomes a life pattern and when you find no satisfaction in your achievements because they only remind you of what's left to achieve.

When you're dedicated to being perfect, you can never be content with what you do. You're constantly critical of yourself and always striving to do better. The pursuit of success doesn't translate into happiness. When success and happiness mean being perfect, problems intensify when a very imperfect world always gets in the way.

What are the things people say as they lie dying? Do they say, "I wish I had impressed my mom"? Probably not, because they said that enough during their life. Do they breathe their last regretting they didn't turn off the porch light or win a Nobel Peace Prize? Bronnie Ware, an Australian songwriter and palliative caregiver, took notes on what her patients said at the end of their lives for her book titled *The Top Five Regrets of the Dying*. Here are two of her entries:

"I wish I'd had the courage to live a life true to myself, not the life others expected of me."

"I wish I had let myself be happier."[1]

Traits of the Perfectionist

The perfectionist finds it difficult to maintain friendships because they see people as having too many problems and faults. Nobody is quite perfect enough. And to complicate things, the perfectionist doesn't believe they are perfect enough to be somebody's friend. One of the items on any happiness scale is "connection," or a gratifying social life. Without this, the perfectionist turns inward and begins to gnaw on their fragile ego like an animal chomps on a wound, which serves to alienate them more.

The perfectionist thinks that happiness is an illusion because the concept of perfection is not compatible with reality. If you look at everything around you, you'll see that most things could probably be improved upon. The room you're in now could probably be decorated better, the car outside could probably use a paint job or at least a wash, the trees in the park probably need some pruning, the building next door may very well need renovating, your shoes may need shining, your nails may need polishing, your hair may need a trim, the work you did yesterday could have been better, the pizza could have been cheesier, the coffee hotter, the sermon shorter—you get the point.

Another kind of perfectionist is the one who takes no chances in life out of fear of making a mistake. This person will never function in extremes or excesses and will choose the middle of the road, where there's the least amount of conflict. A woman I will call Shirley fits this description.

Shirley works hard all year at her job as a bookkeeper in a large corporate real estate business, but when vacation time comes, she doesn't travel somewhere exciting. She stays home and cleans the garage. Last year she rearranged all her bookshelves and cleaned closets. She doesn't hang art on the walls of her house because she doesn't want to make holes in the walls. She hasn't changed her hairstyle since she was in high school twenty years ago, and she doesn't have pets because they're too much responsibility.

Shirley's perfectionism has turned her inside herself. She's so afraid of doing something wrong, making a mistake, or failing that she never tries anything new. Her house, though pristine, lacks personality and flair. Her lifestyle is stilted and pinched. As long as the threat of things not going well lurks in the shadows of her mind, she will never rest in her soul.

Perhaps you're the kind of perfectionist who buries their emotions by working doggedly. If so, you may be using work as an unconscious compensation for your insecurities. Perfectionism may be a means to fulfill your strong needs for approval. You may spend most of your life working at a frantic pace to make a lot of money or to attain power or prestige in order to prove yourself worthy of something, but what you're actually doing is trying to prove yourself to *yourself.* You want to prove to yourself that you aren't the loser-wimp-nobody you suspect you are underneath it all.

I like what a friend of mine did to combat his painful self-demands to succeed, go further, push for more, be spotless and perfect in all he does. When he began jogging, he couldn't run more than two or three hundred yards in the hilly region where he lived without gasping and quitting. Most runners are taught to increase their distance and speed every day, but my friend wanted jogging to be enjoyable, so he decided to run a little *less* two days a week. He laughs when he talks about it because doing less was like swallowing rocks. "I'm the guy who does *more*, not less!" He was determined to enjoy jogging and not make it a grueling and frustrating experience. By doing less two days a week, he removed the pressure he usually put on himself and still accomplished his goal. "Running became enjoyable," he said, "more than I imagined it could be." Over a period of weeks, by daily practice, he built up to the point where he could run seven miles over steep terrain at a fairly rapid pace without his familiar emotional and physical stress. His basic principle, to try to accomplish less two days a week, changed his life.

The Driving Force of Perfectionism

What are the rewards for your dedication to doing everything to perfection? What rewards has perfectionism brought you so far?

Rewards I Think I Get for Being Perfect	Proof That Being Perfect Isn't All That Rewarding
I fulfill God's expectations of me.	I can never fulfill people's expectations, especially God's. Since I can't be perfect, I'm constantly unhappy.

Rewards I Think I Get for Being Perfect	Proof That Being Perfect Isn't All That Rewarding
I fulfill the Scripture passage, "Whatever your hand finds to do, do it with your might" (Eccles. 9:10).	My drive to be perfect makes me competitive, critical, and unloving. I judge other people's performance against what I believe is perfect. I am never happy, even when I do a good job.
I make my parents proud.	I never feel my parents are truly proud, so why am I constantly trying to win their approval? It is God's approval I need, not any person's.
I feel satisfaction in a job well done.	Exhaustion, not satisfaction, is more like it. Besides, I never feel I did a job well enough, no matter how exhausted I am.
People give me respect when I achieve things they admire.	I'm so afraid of making mistakes that I really don't trust the respect people give me. I crave admiration, but when I get it, I don't really believe it's sincere because I'm not perfect.

As the above chart shows, fear always lurks behind the drive to be perfect. Fear will cause you to become a raving obsessive-compulsive person. As you drop your drive to be perfect, you'll have to confront the fear that motivates you. Are criticisms, failure, and disapproval offensive and frightening to you? Does it upset you to think of facing those things? If you insist that everything you do must be just right, you may be motivated by the terror of being criticized or of something bad happening.

Here are behaviors familiar to the perfectionist and how to handle them when they occur. If you don't think you're a perfectionist, consider the following exercise anyway.

1. You're driving in your car, and suddenly you can't remember if you locked your front door at home. Here's the challenge: You must not turn around to check it. Recognize where the

fear is coming from. Recognize your dread of making a mistake. You cannot turn the car around to check your front door. Refuse to do it. Permit yourself to make a mistake. Tell yourself, "I live in the power of the grace of God, and I give myself permission not to be perfect." (I'm not suggesting anything to do with the front door. The front door is not the issue; *you* are the issue, you and your perfectionist motives.)

2. You're at school or work or out with friends, and suddenly you can't remember if you turned the water faucet off in your bathroom. Here's the challenge: If someone is in the house, do not call home. Do not leave to go check. Do absolutely nothing. Notice your agitation. Notice the emotions you're experiencing. Quiet your thoughts, breathe deeply, and pray, "Lord, I give myself permission to make a mistake. I choose to be happy in my skin. I give myself permission not to be perfect." Refuse to give in to your fear of making a mistake no matter how upset you become. It will disappear eventually.

3. Here's the biggie. You've invited friends for dinner. Usually you go to lengthy preparations, but this time you don't cook at all. Instead, serve a feast of take-out ethnic food. Resist the urge to fanatically clean. Don't change clothes. Tell yourself, "I refuse the fear of not doing everything perfectly. I refuse the fear of not having *things* good enough. I am a good host." Your guests will probably have a great time because you'll be so much more relaxed, and you'll be able to concentrate more on them than your dinner.

The fear of doing something wrong or of being found at fault can be overwhelming. It's time to eliminate that fear!

A New View of Life

One of my goals as we work through this book together is to show you that no matter what level of life you're at, no matter what point you're at in your career or family life, your happiness depends on how you see yourself and what you tell yourself. Let me suggest that you make a decision to give up your perfectionism right now, at least on a trial basis.

Hanging on to perfectionism and the misbelief that making mistakes is the end of the world will lead you to procrastinate, quit, run away, or do nothing. This is a formula for depression. Being fixated on perfection can steal your happiness in a number of ways, as with a couple I know who won't have friends over anymore. They don't feel their house is nice enough. Not perfect enough. Since positive socialization is important to a happy life, this couple quarantined themselves inside their house where nothing was perfect enough to share with others.

We're always facing new challenges and experiencing new problems to solve. Believe in the power of the Holy Spirit in you. You have a power in you much greater than you think. Happiness is not possible without growth, and growth starts with looking at and challenging the way you view your life and the world around you. The strengths and stresses of your life are the result of what you have programmed into your belief system. Your views about yourself, about God, about your world, and about what makes life worth living are the forces behind who you are and what you do.

Take notes in your happiness journal as you examine the way you view the events of your life. You can change the amount of stress you suffer by changing your perception of your life and of what makes you valuable.

Before going to the next chapter, let's pause for another five-minute Quiet Prayer exercise. This is a time to practice quieting your mind and emotions, breathe deeply, and allow yourself to be still. Here there are no words, and you simply quiet yourself and focus on being in the presence of God. You're sitting still with Him saying nothing, asking nothing, with no expectations or desires but just to sit with Him. That's why it's called Quiet Prayer. It's an amazing experience, one I hope you will adapt as a daily practice, because happiness is found in inner peace. Are you ready?

Find a quiet place with no distractions and set a timer. Take a deep breath, close your eyes, and allow yourself to rest into your body. Allow yourself time to feel a sense of God's peace in you. God is in the process of making changes in you and bringing you to a higher place of faith. He's with you now. You're in His presence, quiet and still and beautiful.

When the timer sounds, open your eyes, make any notes about your experience in your happiness journal, take another deep breath, and go on to the next chapter.

Holy Awareness

Have you ever started eating a banana and then without barely tasting it you realize it's gone and you're holding the peel? Or have you ever been going somewhere and arrived at your destination only to realize you hardly noticed a thing along the way? This used to happen to me all the time. These are common examples of an awareness deficit. I surprise myself on a regular basis when I notice something that's been there all along but I never really saw it.

We can exist day in and day out without being present in our skin. To be happy, truly happy, a heaping balance of awareness is called for. When I talk about awareness, I mean more than simply being observant. Awareness for our purposes is seeing, hearing, touching, feeling, tasting, and sensing with the mind of Christ. Philippians 2:5 says, "Let this mind be in you which was also in Christ Jesus." This is a verse to take seriously. God formed all creation into being with a thought from His holy mind before calling it into being with the words, "Let there be . . ." And His mind is *in* you.

The mind of Christ in us means we pay attention to what He pays attention to. It means feeling, tasting, touching, listening, seeing, and using all our senses to be aware through Him. I call this holy awareness.

Are you aware of the power of your thought life? Are you *fully* aware of the command to let the mind of Christ dwell (live, exist, thrive) in you? We've built habits of thinking, evaluating, and judging with our human minds, not the mind of Christ. Without holy awareness, we're victims of anxiety, fear, and worry. There's no peace in us because we have no foundation in the mind of Christ.

When we cling to our old learned behaviors and thought patterns, we tend to see life in black-and-white terms—good/bad, righteous/sinful, honest/corrupt, ugly/beautiful, and so on. We live in a chaotic and troubled world, and we can complain all we want, but our complaints and tirades won't change anything or make us better people. Even our prayers can become a relentless cry for God to do something! If we want our prayers to reach the heart of God, we must pray with His mind and know His heart. We must be aware.

It's time to pause, breathe, and look at the world with an altogether new perspective.

Holy Awareness

Awareness of ourselves. If you experienced the two previous five-minute Quiet Prayer sessions, I'm sure you recognized your wild, untamed self-talk and mind clutter. Sitting in stillness with God face-to-face makes you suddenly aware of the frantic swirl of your thought life. You pay attention and become aware of what is going on inside you. Holy awareness begins with self-awareness. From here you begin to make a change. You begin to formulate a new awareness of your need for the mind of Christ to prevail within your spirit.

Awareness of the atmosphere around us. We all have the ability to be present in the moment. By the words "in the moment," I mean being right here right now without your mind wandering, daydreaming, tuning out, avoiding, or denying what's around you right where you are. Become aware of the sounds, movements, actions, sights, and atmosphere immediately surrounding you. The temptation is to look around and find what's wrong, what's missing, what's bad, what's not perfect, what's not right. We can too easily perceive the world around us as a necessary backdrop for a life that we're indifferent to.

An ordinary workday morning for an unaware person might look like this. Get out of bed, shower, get dressed. Get in the car. Drive to work. Park the car. Walk to the coffee shop. Stand in line at the coffee shop and buy a Danish and a latte. Walk back to the office. Get on the elevator. Go to the sixth floor. Arrive at the office.

If someone were to ask if something interesting happened on the way to work, the answer would naturally be no. We can be too busy tuning out. We don't observe the world around us with any interest or appreciation because we're buried inside the dark, dusty hallways of our own heads, and the world around us is only a backdrop.

What a difference it would make if we purposed to be aware of the world around us as we set out on our day! Imagine experiencing and taking mental note of the smells, sounds, and sights surrounding you. Imagine feeling yourself fully alive, appreciating each moment as you go about ordinary tasks. Here's an exercise to try now with this book in your hands. Close your eyes and listen to the sounds around you. Were you aware of them before?

Awareness of the world at large. Anyone can complain about the miserable state of the world. Anyone can rant about the atrocities of terrorism, political corruption, starving nations, evil leaders, media corruption, and rampant immorality, but it's an entirely different thing to sit in stillness and learn from Christ to see with His eyes. Try seeing with eyes that find the good, the beautiful, the blessed.

Practicing Holy Awareness

I teach holy awareness in my happiness classes, and an important foundation session is on being grateful and at peace with all that is presently around us. We learn to accept interruptions and nuisances without judging, getting flustered, or being emotionally disturbed.

One day I was rushing to catch an airplane for a five-day speaking engagement. I was taken by surprise when the counter was closed and I had to haul my two heavy suitcases and my two carry-ons to another counter at the other end of the airport that had to be at least a hundred miles away. To add to the challenge, one of the suitcases had stubborn wheels. I tripped all over it trying to push it, and then I pushed a little too hard and went flying through the air and landed on the floor. I must tell you, I was not in a good mood. Then I heard my own voice in class say, "Holy awareness is a wonderful thing!"

I had to pull myself together there on the floor of the airport, my luggage scattered all around me, and breathe slowly and deeply. If I was going to practice what I preach, I had to get in touch with the situation with an *aware* mind. I spoke to myself in the present tense. "Here you are, Marie, hauling stubborn luggage with cranky wheels in the Orlando airport, and you're enjoying the sound of the crowds, the announcements, the clicking of feet, and the clatter of these wheels. Here you are, Marie, fully experiencing the moment without judgment! Tell yourself the truth, Marie. It's not a bad situation; it's simply a situation." I told myself holy awareness is keeping God company.

I breathed again, chuckled, and arrived at the airline counter, where my assistant was wondering what had happened to me. "I was practicing awareness," I told her.

I tell you this experience because too much of what happens in our lives falls under the category we consider "awful." If something isn't what we want or isn't according to our plans, it's awful. (I still have that suitcase. I stuck a smiley face on its front.)

Be present in all things and be thankful for all things. Being present means to be aware and alive in the moment. It means to pause and feel the air around you, hear the sounds around you, see the movements around you, smell the smells around you. It means touching, tasting, being. Holy awareness floods you with gratitude because it opens your eyes to see with your awakened Christ-filled mind. You're a part of a magnificent, holy plan.

We're quick to judge with "this is bad," and we miss opportunities to be at peace by being present and thankful. As you become more aware with acceptance and gratitude, your entire body sighs with a sigh of peace and contentment. No matter what is going on in the world, you are in the midst of it all and a holy part of God's perfect intention and will. Even falling on your face while yanking stubborn suitcases through a crowded airport when you're late can't rob you of peace.

The Magnitude of Loss

At the core of much of our unhappiness is loss. Something crucial to our well-being is missing. I missed out. I don't have. I lost. I'm not accepted. I'm rejected. I expected but didn't receive. I was passed over. I've been stolen from. They took what was mine. There's no reward. I'm not appreciated. I'm taken for granted. My dream has been shattered. I'm not worthy. I'm a loser. I'm not qualified or equipped enough. I always blow it. I failed. So that makes me a failure.

Let's add, "I feel guilty because—" to the statements above, and they'd ring just as true. "I feel guilty because I missed out." "I feel guilty because I don't have." Loss is one of the tentacles of guilt.

Look at what's missing in your life, something that's important to you. If you don't recognize it and name it, you could become victimized by it. And that victimization includes shards of emotional pain and anger.

How many times are we furious over an injustice or insult and we politely stuff our anger, trying to explain it away by calling it "hurt"? How many times do we depress ourselves because we've turned our anger inside instead of calling it what it is?

Hurt translates into anger. Here's where we need to call on our integrity and spiritual insight to see things clearly for what they are and deal with them in the glare of truth. Anger must be recognized for what it is if we're to move forward toward wholeness and happiness.

A counseling client who was scammed in business by someone he trusted masks his anger with, "I must forgive them. I know God wants me to forgive them."

"Forgiveness given in anger isn't forgiveness. It's getting back at someone," I tell him.

It was important for my client to admit and face his anger toward the people who stole his money, causing him to shut down his business and lose everything he'd built. "I should have seen it coming," he tells me, at last anger rising in his voice. "I was so blind!"

In this book, we're finding God's goodness in all things even when they aren't what we want. This is a process. Falling down in an airport is not the same as losing one's business through betrayal. This is why it's crucial we develop happiness skills in the little things so we can handle the big blows that are flung our way and not allow them to bruise and scar our vulnerable hearts.

The Effects of Anger

Psychological research and statistics illustrate without a shadow of a doubt that anger cannot be successfully denied and buried. Anger will *always* find expression, and if the expression is not handled with the power of the Holy Spirit, it can be devastating. Look, for example, at the number of teen shootings on high school campuses by angry, alienated teen killers. These have been intelligent students who did well and got good grades but were rejected by peers, bullied, picked on. Their rage and repressed anger built in them until they acted out in violence and murder.

Or consider the true-life crime story of Betty Broderick, the San Diego socialite whose husband divorced her and married another woman. Betty up and murdered them both with a gun. The amazing thing is that, fifteen years later while she was locked in a prison cell, Broderick's anger still wasn't quelled. "He deserved it!" she hotly exclaimed to the parole board from behind bars.

Anger and acts of aggression walk arm in arm. Dr. Leonard Berkowitz of the University of Wisconsin has studied the social causes of aggression and said, "When we tell someone off, we stimulate ourselves to continue aggression."[1] We'll do it again, and in time we'll form a habit of telling people off, and we'll excuse ourselves with the lie, "It's just the way I am," followed by, "I can't help it. I'm just being honest with how I feel." Telling someone off, insulting someone, arguing angrily, or allowing a fiery temper to rip is not being honest. It's sin.

Make no mistake. Anger is a killer, and it kills in many ways, not only with murder weapons but also with self-sabotaging behaviors that destroy lives every bit as efficiently as guns. Anger bottled up will eventually erupt in self-denigrating behaviors. Any negative emotion that you keep bottled up is like a poisonous gas gurgling inside you. It will spew out in leaks, which you can recognize by sleep disturbances, eating problems, temper tantrums, lying, pushing too hard for approval, overwork or no work, sexual promiscuity, lethargy, drinking, antisocial behavior, discordant fears, returning to bad habits such as smoking and drugs, verbal abuse, an increase in using bad language, swearing, aggressive behavior, and a desire to hurt someone.

Dealing with Anger

A woman I'll call Sally told me she felt nothing but "understanding and compassion" for a co-worker who, by lying and conniving, landed the promotion that rightfully should have gone to her. She had worked for the company for ten years, worked overtime, never missed a day, took management and leadership courses, got along with everyone, and always went the extra mile, and then someone came along who through underhanded maneuvering nabbed the promotion that should have been hers.

Understanding and compassion? I don't think so. Sally was angry. Anger is not bad in itself, but Sally would lose more than the promotion if she didn't face her feelings square in the eye.

Anger needs to be recognized and handled wisely. In truth, Sally had absolutely *no* understanding or compassion for the situation, but after facing and replacing her nonproductive anger, she began to respect her not-so-pleasant feelings rather than run from them. She learned to say, "It's okay. I'm okay. I let go."

God wants you whole. He wants you to be a healthy, vibrant, beautiful human being. He wants to show you how to step aside and respond to injustice and the cares of life with peace in your heart. You have a right to your feelings. By denying anger, you rob yourself of being a complete human being. Anger can be painful, but these feelings won't kill you.

The old-school ideas of dealing with anger by getting alone and screaming or punching something do not work. Screaming and punching don't eliminate angry feelings. Such activities just teach you to scream and punch things.

You may also have heard it said that any angry arousal will eventually diminish if you just wait long enough. It'll eventually go away on its own. Not true. In a world filled with unhappiness, cruelty, violence, poverty, war, and terrorism, anger does not diminish by itself. It multiplies. Anger is fuel for the fire of hate. Anger and hatred live inside a person and inside the heart of a nation.

Most theories now point to the fact that anger and its expression are a result of choice. To change, we must face our emotions and make new choices when handling them. The first choice is to stop denying the feeling.

When we realize it's our perceptions, our attitudes, and our self-talk that control our emotions and not people, situations, or events, we can begin the journey to inner freedom.

Let me give you an example: "I was fired for something I didn't do. That's rotten, terrible, and unforgivable, and I'm furious!" You can almost feel the person's body tense up, the eyes water, the fingers knot into fists.

Observe the running inner dialogue: "That's rotten, terrible, and unforgivable, and I'm furious."

Examine the words of that sentence without judgment. This brings clarity.

Respond with mercy and clarity. "Okay. It's not fair that I was fired for something I didn't do. My world won't end because of it. Remaining furious will destroy me."

Replace the self-talk. "I'm choosing to turn this around and hold to the truth that God is working all things together for my good. I declare as Joseph did to his brothers, 'What you meant for evil, God has turned to good.' I will allow myself the right to feel angry, but I'm in control, not my feelings, and I choose to have faith in God's justice through this experience."

There was no denial of anger but instead intelligent and holy management of a challenge.

Here are four simple anger-management tools.

1. When you're out somewhere among people and something ticks you off, be quiet and calm your mind before speaking or doing anything. If it's possible without being obvious, remove yourself from the situation to be alone for a few minutes to talk to yourself. Close your eyes and take some long, slow breaths. It's impossible to act out in anger while breathing deeply. Speak the Word of God to yourself. Give yourself time to *choose* your response.

2. Be unafraid to talk about angry feelings. Discuss your feelings rather than act them out on people. Admit the anger and

tell yourself you are not a bad person for feeling angry. It's far healthier to say, "I feel angry right now" than to spout out with hostility you'll regret later. When discussing your feelings, remember that nobody else is the cause. You choose your feelings.

3. Eliminate from your vocabulary misbeliefs such as, "You make me angry!" Not true. People can't make you angry. Situations can't make you angry. The truth is you make yourself angry. The choice is yours. You listen and react to your perception of what's being said or done, and you make yourself angry.

4. Once you understand that you make yourself angry, begin the process of going deeper inside to learn more of the truth about yourself. You have so much more beauty within than you're aware of. Inside you is a golden well of wonderfulness that is God Himself. Tap into Him and the loveliness within you.

Frustration is a first cousin of anger, and they work in tandem. Here are exercises to help you deal with frustration.

1. Understand and accept that it's okay to be frustrated. You won't always be. You'll look back and be able to say you handled it well. Frustration is not your master.

2. Be aware of your identity, who you are in the eyes of God and in the eyes of all heaven. This takes some effort on your part. It takes getting quiet before the Lord and opening the pages of His Word and meditating on what you read.

3. Fall in love with the truth. Jesus said "You shall know the truth, and the truth shall make you free" (John 8:32). Notice He said you will *know* the truth before He said it will make you free. You can't be set free from unsettling, unhappy emotions without knowing inside, deeply and truly, what is the truth. You can recite positive affirmations until you see pink

twinkle dust, but without the solid foundation of the truth as God has revealed it, you will never be completely free.

4. Become dedicated to engaging in a new form of self-talk. To end the cycle of negative, defeating words that continually harangue your thoughts and behavior, begin to let a new language guide you. This new language is one with your body, soul, and spirit. Listen to your heart's voice. See yourself as being an important part of the omnipotent, omnipresent, omnificent heart of God. You're embedded in His eternal, perfect heart. He holds you in the palm of His hand, and He has infused His Holy Spirit into your human spirit. Inside you are the heart and soul of eternal God Himself.

Loss and Betrayal

We need to erase from our minds that happiness is situational. We're glad and grateful for every beautiful thing and person in our lives, and our gratitude feeds our sense of well-being. This is good! But when the things and people we're grateful for are no longer there, what happens? If you're like most of us, you become disillusioned, hurt, lost, *unhappy*. The emotional degree of your reaction, of course, depends on the circumstances of the loss. If you're a wife and your husband of twenty-five years suddenly leaves you for another woman and demands a divorce, you're going to suffer the loss differently than the woman whose husband left her through an untimely death.

Through the loss of a precious love and the hope of a future togetherness, I had to teach myself lessons learned only in sorrow. Through the loss of both my parents and mourning pitifully, I had to teach myself how to live again, honoring life and a purpose for being here.

Then came betrayal. Betrayal is a terrible kind of loss. It's the loss of dignity. It's the rape of the soul. When we're betrayed, especially by someone we trusted, something in us dies. And we grieve our own death. In time, we become wiser, no longer so naïve, no longer so filled with faith in people. Our beautiful, open-minded, wide-eyed, trusting hearts are muddied. Betrayal is a terrible kind of loss, and we must rush to grab hold of the words Joseph spoke to his brothers and make them ours: "You meant evil against me; but God meant it for good" (Gen. 50:20). Grab those words, hug them tightly, and love them! Shout out, "Death, where is your sting?" (1 Cor. 15:55). "Not here! I am whole and complete in Christ!" (see Col. 2:10).

Some people never recover from betrayal. They become bitter, guarded, angry people. They shrink from life's wondrous challenges and hide out in the shadows of their wounded egos. By the same token, some people never recover from loss, whatever it might be. They live in a well of self-pity, never reaching their full potential or experiencing life in all its miraculous fullness because grief has them by the neck and won't let go. The apostle Paul wrote how they were persecuted, betrayed, murdered, and ground to dust, yet they rejoiced. They weren't destroyed or defeated (see 2 Cor. 4:8–9).

The widow or widower is faced with a challenge—that of carrying on through the loss of a loved one and the loss of a lifestyle shared with another person. How can they be happy when they have lost their love? Almost everyone has experienced a breakup of a close relationship, which is painful enough, but death is world-jolting and numbing to the one left behind.

The arms of God open wide to enfold us in our grief. He soothes us, kisses our tears, and builds us up to see a world completely new and all ours to inhabit and make beautiful. It's time to look up and see the glory of the stars in the sky and thank God.

Praise and Happiness

One of your best happiness skills is making the decision to praise the Lord no matter what's going on in your life, no matter what you have lost. Gratitude chases away negative emotions like nothing else. Thanking God for the good in your life is a balm, an elixir, a healing tool that is better than any human remedy on earth.

I've been in Nigeria as part of an evangelistic team, and on Sunday mornings we worshiped with the local church outside in the blinding African heat. The people praised the Lord by the hour! The people sang—no, they *shouted*—glorious songs of worship, repeating the words over and over again. Instruments of all kinds played in the heat, and on and on we praised, voices swelling and crescendoing beyond our mortal selves. Here in this Third World environment, sweltering in oppressive heat and poverty, hundreds of believers gathered to praise God.

My role on the ministry team was teaching the women's classes and leading prayer meetings. I know many of their personal stories. I know how one woman's husband beat her senseless on a regular basis, how another woman gave her milk for other women's babies for money in order to live. I know about their sicknesses, the multiple-wife situations, the tribal fighting, the wars, the political upheavals, the drug and alcohol issues. Yet there they were, praising God and worshiping Him with all their energy and all their might on broiling hot Sunday mornings. They worshiped and praised God *in spite of* and through their hardships.

In our lives and our losses, if we stop praising God, we lose sight of our true selves. We praise Him in various ways, whether shouting and dancing or quietly worshiping Him or sitting with Him in Quiet Prayer. Praise is our release from all suffering. When you feel weighted down, pull out Psalm 150 and begin to praise the Lord. Praise Him with Psalm 103 (my favorite): "Bless the LORD, O my soul; and all that is within me, bless His holy name!" (v. 1).

Anger doesn't exist in your feet or your earlobes. It is inside you, inside your heart. You also have love in your heart, but it can get pushed out. You also have joy, peace, and forgiveness in your heart. Take part in a five-minute Quiet Prayer. Allow what's beautiful in you to overtake that which is ugly and deadly. Allow the beautiful One in you to overtake your entire being.

Every aspect of God's presence is accessible to you. As you draw aside to be alone with God, the nearness of His presence will become blinding in its glory over time, and then slowly the truth will capture your heart. When the truth that sets you free permeates your mind and becomes a part of you, you're saturated consciously and unconsciously. You and the truth become one. It's then that you are made free. The arms of happiness wrap around you, and there are no more words. The sense of loss loses its grip and its sting.

Quiet Prayer

For this Quiet Prayer, select a word, phrase, or Bible passage that will be your sacred word. Speak your word silently to yourself, then set your timer and close your eyes. Take some nice, deep breaths and focus on being alone with God. Every time your mind wanders or the chatter in your mind begins, simply acknowledge the thought and return to your sacred word.

After the five minutes are up, take a deep breath, open your eyes, and say your word out loud. If you like, make a note in your happiness journal about what you experienced in the silence before going on to the next chapter.

As you return to your normal activities, try to continue the quieting of your mind. Be aware of the chatter that constantly goes on inside, and be aware that the secret place of the Most High is always waiting for you to return.

The Search for Success
in an Unhappy World

Joe, a successful attorney, distinguished for his integrity and sound legal knowledge, had just won the primary in an election to be the judge in his county. He said, "I was more surprised by how little the victory meant. It left me feeling empty inside." You'd think Joe would have felt happy about his success, but he was deeply burdened after his win and couldn't sleep at night. After much prayer, reading the Word, soul-searching, and spiritual counseling, he surprised everyone with a decision. Joe, the good judicial candidate, decided to become a priest.

Father Joseph says now, "I'm so much more satisfied with my life. I know the true feeling of happiness. I'd rather wear a clerical collar than a judge's robe, and I'm happy driving a used VW van instead of my Rolls." He tells me he's found true meaning and happiness helping others find and know God. He responded to God's call to something higher than the world's idea of success.

There are countless definitions of success, large and small. The other day I overheard a woman raving ecstatically that her puppy had finally learned to go pee-pee on the paper. "Success is ours!" she gleefully announced.

Most dictionaries define *success* as the favorable termination of a venture, "the achieving of desired results, or someone or something that achieves positive results."[1] We feel we've achieved success at the progressive realization of a worthy ideal. There are many ways to look at success.

A hospitalized patient says, "Success is when I stop hurting."

Others may say, "Success is being able to pay all the bills each month." "Success is getting a passing grade in statistics." "Success is acceptance into the college I want." "Success is when the printer works." "Success is when I can sleep an entire night through."

Does success make you happy, or does happiness make you successful? I believe the latter.

Success is a process more than a realization, and we're rarely as successful as we think we should be. Even more rare is finding *meaning* in what we consider success. The concept of happiness has been extensively analyzed by philosophers, psychologists, scientists, and historians. Throughout history, happiness often centered on good luck and fortune, whereas in modern times, particularly in the West, happiness is viewed more as something over which we have control or can pursue. We achieve a worthy goal and we are considered successful; therefore we should be happy. Not so.

Philosophers and religious leaders often define happiness in terms of living a good life, of flourishing, but it's not possible to live a good life and flourish if we aren't happy first. Therefore, the philosophy has holes in it.

I love the story found in the fifteenth-century Jewish classic *Orchos Tzaddikim* that says a person is obligated to bless the Almighty for misfortune with the same joy as when they bless the Lord for good fortune. The story tells how two rabbinic students asked the Maggid of Mez'ritch, the wise and noble leader and teacher, how this was possible. The Maggid advised them to ask Rabbi Zushe, who was extremely poor and lacked even basic necessities. He lived a thoroughly impoverished and difficult life of many troubles, yet he always seemed happy. The students went to the study hall, where they found the rabbi and told him the Maggid had said he would explain how it was possible to bless the Almighty with joy over misfortune.

"I'm surprised that our Rabbi sent you to me about this," he replied. "You should ask someone who has suffered some misfortune in his life. I have never experienced anything bad in my life. Only good things have happened to me."[2]

So much sweeter is the success that flows naturally from the core of the happy heart.

The French poet who coined the word *surrealism*, Guilaume Apollinaire, said, "Now and then it's good to pause in our pursuit of happiness and just be happy."[3]

We think we'll be happy when we reach a certain goal or when we're basking in the acceptance and praise of others. We think we'll be happy when we have more than what we have right now. I like what one American journalist said: "We are seldom happy with what we now have, but would go to pieces if we lost any part of it."

Does our annual income reflect success? Studies have been conducted regarding annual income, and respondents said they would choose a lower income as long as it was higher than their neighbors' instead of a higher income that was less than their neighbors'. So they would prefer an annual income of $40,000 if their neighbor made $35,000 over making $60,000 if their neighbor made $70,000.

Success and Responsibility

Let's look at one of the problems success brings us all: responsibility. If you win a trophy for your gymnastic skills, or you land a college scholarship, or you get a raise in salary, or you give birth, you're responsible to bear the expectations of that event. Even the woman whose puppy learned to be paper trained now had the responsibility to take her pet to the *next* level of training.

The thrill of a single achievement fades quickly. The writer with her first successful novel is now responsible for her next novel, and will it be as good as the first? A successful businessman or woman is responsible for maintaining and exceeding their initial levels of success.

I've observed in the counseling room that the achievement of success can make a person reactive, not creative. Many famous people fear their own success, and self-destruction often underlies the most profound accolades. Ernest Hemingway, the author who committed suicide, as had his father before him, was never satisfied with the literary achievements that had made him famous. His many other achievements in life didn't bring him the satisfaction he craved either. At the end of his life, he demanded of himself that he write better, hunt better, fish better, and be an altogether better macho image. He didn't regard the success he had achieved as valuable.

Some people don't try to achieve a dream or a goal because the fears of responsibility and failure are just too great. The person who is motivated by low self-esteem to prove themselves to others by succeeding experiences a painful struggle. They may abandon the pursuit along the way, and often just at the crest of succeeding. This is often what happens to the EBT doctoral candidate, that is, Everything But the Thesis candidate. The idea is, "I'll do it later." But later doesn't usually come. "Success can so easily be lost. I better not go there. To fall from success would be terrible" is the misbelief.

Sometimes the pressure to succeed can be so great that even the best of the best will sometimes up and quit what they've worked so hard to achieve.

I spent the early years of my life in the theater, and I once worked with a pianist I'll call Jeffrey. He was the pianist in the orchestra of the musical I was playing in. He took the job in our orchestra to make extra money, but his real goal was to be a solo concert pianist. He was just twenty years old, had won awards as a protégé, and now was determined to make it on the solo concert circuit. He landed a good manager and had some concert bookings already on his calendar. A lifetime of hard work, study, perseverance, and arduous daily practice were finally paying off. Then one day, out of the blue, he quit playing! He simply slammed the lid of his Steinway and refused to play again. At the very apex of attaining his dream of glory, he turned his back and at this writing has not played again.

Jeffrey's reason for quitting? While rehearsing a rigorously demanding piece by Rachmaninoff, he made so many mistakes that he hit the keys with his fist and stomped off in a panic. It wasn't the first time he had punched the keys angrily at a mistake, but this time his panic was so severe that he froze. He saw it as the beginning of the end, and no one could convince him otherwise. Jeffrey's self-worth was sealed in the excellence of his performance alone.

You lose a lot when your definition of success is based on all-or-nothing thinking. Success based on achievement may only drive you to work harder to try to recapture the feeling you once had. Achievement often compels people to achieve more.

There's one more category of people I want to talk about, because in spite of our changing world and great strides made in our modern Western culture, there are certain women who still fit into the fear-of-success classification due to their fear of losing their ability to be loved by men. They've identified with their role as the "weaker sex" and have not taken into account that men and women are "joint heirs in Christ" (Rom. 8:16–17). The notion of weakness has erroneously been interpreted as "inept." This misbelief says a woman should remain inept, not too smart, not too successful, not too capable if she wants to be loved by a man. This idea promotes the attitude that success and achievement are somehow unfeminine. Tell that to the female soldiers, scientists, bank presidents, doctors, financial moguls, and business owners. Tell that to the Proverbs 31 woman. Tell it to the women of the Bible, from Sarah to Deborah to Hannah to Queen Esther to Elizabeth to Mary to Lydia to Priscilla—all married, all loved by men.

Happiness as the Foundation for Success

We have a misconception that success in life is based on getting, on receiving, but a Harvard Business School study found that spending money on others actually makes us happier than spending it on ourselves.

I know three PhDs who aren't pursuing their chosen fields. One works as a short-order cook in a tiny restaurant in New York City. Another is selling real estate in Palm Springs. The third decided to be a stay-at-home dad. Yet all three are leading *happy* lives today. They made conscious decisions to examine their ideas of success. They chose to listen to their hearts and to base the nucleus of their happiness on who they *are*, not on what they *do*. And that is the point. God is calling us to *be*.

Knowing yourself means knowing who you are in God and who He is in you. No one else can tell you your calling. It comes from within you, from God Himself. Proverbs 3:13 says, "Happy is the man who finds wisdom, and the man who gains understanding." Such wisdom and understanding apply first to who you are in Christ, because all your decisions, ideas, thoughts, and desires come from that place.

The lovely, gentle, big-hearted souls who bring life and beauty to the world from the inside out radiate God's goodness. These individuals are happy with who they are in the world, and happiness doesn't depend on whether or not you and I like them or accept them. They have found and know the Source of lasting happiness. "Happy are the people whose God is the LORD" (Ps. 144:15).

Without happiness at its base, success is shallow and fleeting. It's why so many people at the top of their game crash.

The apostle Paul was an example for us who believe. We can endure all things. That's *all* things. "I have learned," Paul wrote, "in whatsoever state I am, therewith to be content" (Phil. 4:12 KJV). The Good News Translation reads, "I know what it is to be in need and what it is to have more than enough. I have learned this secret, so that anywhere, at any time, I am content" (Phil. 4:12).

This verse can also apply to our mental states. "I have learned in whatsoever emotional hassle I'm in to be content." Deep in you is the willingness to let go. You have contentment within you. Quiet yourself and go there.

Sometimes our definitions of success are beyond reality. Not all people helpers can work as hard as others without burning out or losing their joy. Exhaustion is a sure killer of enthusiasm. Enthusiasm is a critical component to our happiness. It feeds us, nourishes us, and energizes us. People in the helping professions are especially prone to overdoing and missing out on the fulfillment that self-sacrifice is supposed to bring.

For the person who believes they can create significant change in the world, they need to have a holy direction from a higher motivating force, one higher than their own sheer grit and determination. Jesus said, "Without Me you can do nothing" (John 15:5), and when we take his words seriously, the fog begins to part from before our eyes, and we see more clearly into His purposes.

When Success Is All-Important

Do you know someone who sees himself or herself as the most important person on the planet? This person usually insists others get on their bandwagon and support their work or their vision. They don't recognize people's value outside of their own needs and demands. This kind of thinking reflects something called narcissism.

Such people believe they're superior to everyone and have little regard for anyone else's feelings. This doesn't mean they have high confidence. On the contrary, their showy, inflated sense of confidence is a mask for their fragile, low self-esteem, and they can't handle the slightest criticism.

These unhappy people crave their idea of success above all else. Politics, the arts, and sports are typical areas of pursuit where the misbelief of being more important than others outweighs all else. The narcissist simply cannot lose. To lose would mean they are worse than nothing; mistakes are intolerable.

You can understand how such misbeliefs are birthed and nourished. We're taught from the time we're children to dream big, to think outside the box, to go for the gold, to reach for the stars, and we can confuse God's voice with platitudes, positive thinking, and advertising slogans. We don't pause to consider that our little self-made kingdom we're striving to build could destroy us.

In the sports world, self-absorption is ubiquitous. But even in highly competitive sports, there are those who choose the higher road and keep God at the center of their lives. Take Missy Franklin, a former Olympic swimmer now turned pro, who at age seventeen won five Olympic medals, four of which were gold. As of this writing, she has won twenty-two medals in international competition—fourteen gold, five silver, and three bronze.

Her goal, she says, is to show the world what God has done in her life. "God is always there for me. I talk with Him before, during, and after practice and competitions. I pray to Him for guidance. I thank Him for this talent He has given me and promise to be a positive role model for young athletes in all sports."[4] She's the opposite of narcissists who crave success for themselves.

Success Not Based on Happiness

When I was a teenager training daily in ballet and jazz dance classes, it was common to hear fellow dancers curse themselves in frustration at some mistake in movement, leap, or turn. Maybe the shameful error was a spin on the toe not finished smoothly or a leap that didn't quite soar high or light enough. It was not unfamiliar for a principal dancer to curse herself for a mistake and bring the entire rehearsal to a stop.

One of the teachers I had the privilege to study with was the great Russian prima ballerina Alexandra Danilova. She led our classes with a long stick in her hand, which she tapped constantly throughout the workout. She would whap our legs to correct our position as we went through our *barre* exercises.

Once out on the center floor, we would follow her instructions perfectly, and so intense was our concentration that if we were the tiniest bit off in our movements, we felt somehow disgraced. The ones in the front of the class were the examples, the "favorites," the best. I was one of those choice ones, and so I was more driven, more intense.

It wasn't that we were happy when we did well; it was more that we escaped being miserable at *not* doing well. Everything was contingent upon performance.

Class never ended for me. At home in my room, I would practice my turns, my point work, trying to perfect the smallest detail of movement. I stretched and pulled and yanked and starved and sweat until I believed there was nothing in the world that could interfere with attaining the terrible goals I had set for myself.

Steve Jobs said, "The only way to do great work is to love what you do. Don't settle." He spoke of work as a "matter of the heart."[5]

Yes, I loved God. Yes, I loved my mom, my dad, my sister and brother, and other people, but I was obsessed with dance. Obsessions aren't always vehicles leading the way toward success and certainly not toward happiness. The paradox is that obsession is applauded and necessary for excellence in most endeavors.

In show business and the arts, not being the best, or wildly innovative, or magically creative can mean *unemployment*. Excellence isn't bad in itself, but to some people it's their barometer for success. There is no in-between, no relief from joyless demands.

Not being the best doesn't mean being second best; it means being the worst.

On and on the work to achieve, to excel, continues, and harder and harder it becomes. Nothing satisfies the achiever because there's always more to achieve. This is not success based on happiness.

Success and Purpose

How do you express happiness? What do you love to do when you're feeling happy? (Not what you do *to* feel happy.) How is your beautiful happiness seen by the world around you?

God has given each of us a calling. It's what is known as "purpose." In chapter 2, I talked about your life's vision, which is the same as your calling and purpose. It's up to you to find that calling. You may not be called to the priesthood, or to run a soup kitchen, or to dance with the American Ballet Theatre, but it may be to drive a school bus in Kansas City and to be a blessing to the schoolkids every day. It may be to teach fitness classes to unbelievers and lead them to Jesus. It may be to flip hamburgers in McDonald's and bring some light there. It may be to lead Bible studies to men and women in prison.

Human beings are created for purpose. Our purpose can change depending on the stage of life we're in. One of my college professors half-jokingly told us of his concern that his department chairperson was going to retire him at his next birthday, and sure enough, it happened. The professor simply couldn't handle the concept of finding a new purpose. He wasn't interested in what he saw retirement as: hobbies, travel, volunteering, or sitting by the pool. He had no idea what to do with himself without his job. He died a year later.

My professor lost his purpose. It's heartbreaking because this is one of the biggest lies anyone could ever fall for. God calls each of us to not one but many purposes. You need to believe what you do is important, no matter what it is. Everything you touch is sacred. Treat yourself with the dignity God treats you with. If you resent the success of others, it indicates you don't value what you do and you'll be miserable no matter how productive you are. When it becomes clear to you how important you are to God and *His* purposes, you'll realize that you are successful. My professor couldn't see his total potential. He had no idea that his life could begin anew with his retirement from his teaching job.

Lasting happiness requires a belief in your purpose.

Here's an exercise for your happiness journal: Name four purposes you know God has for your life. Not one, four.

Make Yours a Success Story

What happens to the achievers who conquer their self-inflated striving for achievement? They take a good look at their happiness skills. They become like Phil Mahre, the Olympic ski racer who won the title of greatest US skier of all time in 2002. His life took a complete turnaround when his first baby boy was born while he was in Sarajevo winning the men's slalom at the winter Olympics. He chose to settle down and get out of the hoopla, and told the world at the age of twenty-six that he was retiring. He decided what counted most for him was his family, and ski racing dropped down from first place to second. He had won three consecutive World Cup titles, a streak that is equivalent to winning three Super Bowl titles.[6] He and his twin brother, Steve, also a champion skier, now operate the Mahre Ski Training Center in Deer Valley, Utah.

Phil Mahre's story is a success story because he looked at his life and recognized what really mattered to him. He dared to follow his heart! Can you dare to see yourself outside your achievements?

Here's a verse that pertains directly to your success in life: "Beloved, I pray that you may prosper in all things and be in health, just as your soul prospers" (3 John 2). To prosper means to flourish, bloom, succeed in material terms, be financially successful, grow physically strong and healthy, thrive, and progress. Let's translate the verse like this: "May you be as successful as your soul is successful."

Your soul comprises your intellect, your emotions, and your will, each of which is a gift from God. When you use the gift of your intellect to do something wonderful for God, your soul prospers. When you give your emotional life to Him, your soul prospers. When you choose His way above your self-centered way, your soul prospers.

The word *prosper* is also often translated as "good." Goodness is a magnet for blessings. Psalm 25:12–13 tells us that the one who fears (loves and respects) the Lord will dwell in prosperity (goodness). The goodness you attract when your soul is filled with God prospers you in every way. Your soul prospers when your intellect, your emotions, and your will are completely dedicated to God, filled with Him, motivated by Him, and producing life through Him. The prospering of the soul is a *total* prospering. It's the process we're learning in this book. Total prospering = lasting happiness.

Psychoanalyst Dr. Edmund Bergler had a field guide for discovering when we're likely to hurt ourselves by pursuing goals.[7] I've used his ideas as the basis for the following questions:

1. Do you have a contempt for moderate earnings?
2. Do you have high ambitions that lead you to take huge risks?
3. Do you have an exaggerated sense of success combined with a tendency to overwork?
4. Do you have a propelling drive toward more and more "success"?
5. Are you dissatisfied and bored when deprived of fresh business excitement and opportunities to show off?
6. Do you have a cynical outlook plus hypersensitivity and super-suspiciousness?

7. Are you contemptuous and impatient in your attitudes toward unsuccessful people?
8. Do you have an I-know-better attitude, and are you discontent with the simple pleasures of life?
9. Do you have hidden doubts about yourself and your abilities to maintain your level of achievement?
10. Do you enjoy having a grandiose air of importance?

If you can answer yes to two or more of these questions, you need to give your drive to prosper to God so you can work it out in the greatness of His Spirit. Your attitudes toward success and failure may be corroded with confused ideas. Your drive for approval may be excessive.

Here are some questions for your happiness journal:

1. How will you work at prospering your soul: your intellect, your emotions, your will?
2. How will the prospering of your soul bring you success?
3. Why do you want to be a success?
4. What will it take to compromise your values?

God wants you to know what He considers success. Pause here and meditate on the words, "Seek your happiness in the LORD, and He will give you your heart's desire" (Ps. 37:4 GNT). Then read Psalm 1 and know that He wants you to be like a tree planted by the rivers of water, prospering in all you do. Sense His presence very near.

Work and Happiness

Are success and happiness compatible, or are they mutually exclusive?

Bishop T. D. Jakes says that success never feels like success. What you dreamed of and what you later achieve feel like two separate things.

I sat at lunch with the president of a large, multimillion-dollar company and asked her what her definition of success is. "Success is happiness," she answered without a pause. "Money is important," she said, chewing on an olive from her niçoise salad, "but it has to be looked at in perspective. I tell my sons to work toward doing a good job. If we do the very best we can, someone will notice us. A person doing a good job won't go unnoticed."

I listened, waiting for more. She went on. "I thought hitting the top meant to have the world on a string. I come from the hood, and as a kid we were dirt poor, so I always believed having money was the key to happiness. Owning things, not worrying about bills. Ha! I have more bills now than dogs have fleas. I know

now that happiness doesn't have much to do with your position or with money."

I asked her what kinds of things she worries about, if she ever worries about losing her job. Does she lose sleep over her responsibilities? Does she worry about the company's competition? "Oh, sure, I worry," she said with a laugh, "but it doesn't help me do my job any better. I have to concentrate on what works, not on what doesn't. Besides, my job and the company aren't the most important things in my life.

"If I'm a success, it's because I have found favor in the sight of the Lord and I please Him. Not only in work but also in my home, my family, my community, and my church, I try to make my life calling to please Him."

A life calling to please the Lord.

"And how does this make you happy?" I asked.

Her voice softened. She leaned toward me and said, "Marie, when I was a young, inexperienced, shy, and scared kid doing a job I wasn't qualified for at another company, I gave my life to Christ. We all have these big holes in us only God can fill, and He filled the hole in me. I asked Jesus to commandeer my life. He showed me I am no more important to Him where I'm at now than when I was a poor kid living in the hood."

In the self-discovery survey I conducted, 30 percent of the four hundred respondents reported they were in work situations they didn't particularly like. Some said they stayed in the job because it paid good money. Others stayed in unhappy job situations because of the economy and a fear of not finding another job, others because they were afraid to lose their retirement, others because of a lack of skills to get a better job, and still others because of a fear of the unknown. The responses were mainly fear based.

Why do we do the work we do? Why do we stay in the work we do? We're fast becoming an information society, and it's vital that you and I see where we belong in it. A secret of staying happy is to recognize and accept change and progress around you with the mind and heart of God. What is He saying to you? How is He leading and guiding you? God will always invest in His purposes. If you're aligned with the purposes of God, you'll always prevail because God always invests in Himself.

If you believe that God always invests in His purposes, why would you still want to pursue your own purposes?

Right Where You Are and Doing What You Do

Peter made his living as a fisherman. It was his career, his field of expertise, his job. About a week after Jesus was crucified, Peter, still grieving, went fishing, doing what he knew how to do. He took six other men with him and fished all night, but they caught nothing. Sometimes you'll find that when you're doing the work you're called to do, the rewards just aren't there right away. You catch nothing. You work hard, you fish all night, and you catch nothing. Morning dawns, and not a single fish flaps in your net.

It's during those discouraging times that you wonder if your calling is real. You're tempted to wonder if you're in the right career. Maybe God didn't call you after all. You're tempted to downgrade your work, dishonor your work.

Honoring your work and working hard are two different things. You can work hard and hate your job. When you honor your work, you show respect for yourself and for God, who wants to bless and prosper you. Honor yourself and your work. This is soul work (mind, emotions, and will). It takes a decision and effort on your part; it takes your intention.

Out on the water, Peter heard a voice calling from the shore. "Children, have you any food?" (John 21:5). I ask you, what grown man calls grown men "children"? Only a parent! This term of endearment is what a father calls his sons. Some translations have the word *lads*, *boys*, or *sons*. John recognized Jesus first, but only after Jesus told them to cast the net over the right side of the boat—which they did, and the net filled with so many fish they couldn't even haul it in—did he get the whole picture.

Think what would have happened if Peter had ignored Jesus's suggestion to cast the net on the other side of the boat and just sat there bemoaning his life. Jesus wants to bless your work. He blessed Peter at his job! Jesus wants to bless you with miracles and more fish (blessings) than you can haul in, but perhaps you're too wrapped up in trying to bless yourself and work your own miracles.

God wants to show you where to cast your net. He'll honor you right where you are. As His "boys" made their way to shore, shocked and completely beside themselves, they towed a burgeoning net filled with 153 fish, a huge haul! God wants to bless you in your work, and not in dribbles with little toss-'em-back fish. Jesus shared the bounty by sitting down and having a fish-fry breakfast with the men. In fact, He already had the fire going before they reached Him.

Let go of your fears, your worries, and all of the doubts that harass your soul and mess up your work. Throw your net over on the other side. Throw in your line. Let it go deep. Walk by faith, not by sight. Let go and watch for the miracles. You might have to wait all night through what is called "the dark night of the soul," so I say do it with gratitude. Don't waste an opportunity to outdo and outsmart your selfish, complaining self with the power of gratitude. If you're out in the dark on the lake with no fish, enjoy the night sky. Look up at the stars. Sing. Recite Scripture. Think creatively and praise God. Expect a miracle.

And let go of jealousy. Let go of striving. Let go of competing. Let go of lying. Let go of worrying about the future. Let go of feeling you missed the boat. God has miracles ahead for you.

The Lord honored Peter's work that day with a miracle of bounty, and He wants to do the same for you. Honor your work right where you are. If you do what it takes to honor and prosper your soul, God will always honor you and your work.

Integrate the following tools into your daily life and know that what you're doing now is meaningful.

Take a wider view of life around you. See yourself, your family, your community, and your church with a new perspective. See yourself as a part of something much larger than your own small world. Allow your world to expand. In this way, your mind is loosed from the pinched claw of your needs.

Honor your feelings and then let them go. See yourself as whole. See yourself as a person of faith and courage. I'm not suggesting you deny feelings of fear and doubt, but when you feel these things, acknowledge the feelings and then let them go. Your emotions don't possess you. Honor them and then release them from the truth in your core. The Holy Spirit is in you; He's your Helper, your Friend, sent from God in the name of Jesus to make all things plain to you (John 14:26).

Embrace the moment. Don't lose this moment if it isn't exactly what you want. We lose way too much of our lives by waiting for better things to take place in the future. "To everything there is a season, a time for every purpose under heaven" (Eccles. 3:1), and the season in this moment is yours not to discount or to elude but to embrace. This very season, this very *moment* you're living in right now is yours in all its wonder and in all its difficulty and complexity.

Honor your work right where you are. Prosper your soul and let God prosper your work. Love what God sees in you right where you are.

Dreams

How many of your lifelong dreams and desires can you name? (A desire is different from a goal. A goal has a time limit and an accomplishment factor. If, say, you vow to read ten books by August, that's a goal. But if you want to start reading more, that's a desire.) Take out your happiness journal and make the list as lengthy as you can, going back to the dreams you had for your life as a child as well as the most recent ones you had as an adult. Next, rank the dreams in order of their importance to you. What do your dreams say about you? Why have some remained dreams and not become *goals* before now?

The Inner Need for More

The first sign that something is off-kilter in your life is when your desires are more important than your quest for God. I know what that's like. I was there. I've already shared with you how, as a young person, I lived and breathed my love for ballet and the theater. My dream in life was to dance, and I gave all my energy and heart to a career. I danced my way through high school and performed regularly in USO shows, with local theater companies, with the Midwest Ballet Company, on TV, at trade shows, and in musicals before heading to New York City to study professionally and to work. I squeezed God in where He fit with my dreams. I didn't really know how far away from Him I was because spiritually I wasn't very developed. I had given my life to the Lord at a Baptist prayer meeting when I was twelve. I was a Christian, yes, but my work was my religion, and I loved it with a religious passion. God was so merciful to me because He saw what I couldn't see. He saw how desperately I needed Him, and He made me recognize that need. I, too, had that God-shaped hole in me that only He could fill.

One summer I was visiting my family in Minnesota, and I saw the lives of my Christian aunts and uncles who loved God and seemed to radiate with happy, fulfilled lives. Their lives just looked bright to me, but I was into positive thinking and Zen at the time, nothing to do with Jesus, even though I considered myself a good Christian. My sister took me by the shoulders and said, "Marie, the way to God is through *Jesus*." I thought the roof had fallen on my head. I didn't know what to do; I could hardly move. I managed to wend my way to a quiet place in the house and sit alone in the dark. I sat there in the quiet and the stillness, and then out loud in the dark I said yes—yes to Jesus.

From that moment, my world has never been the same. A giant explosion took place inside me. The Holy Spirit moved into me, and my spirit fused with His. It was shocking, earth-rattling. I knew my life had been split open. I told my uncle the next day I was not going back to New York the same person. Up to that point, I had listened to hundreds of sermons based on being good and living the Golden Rule, but I didn't know how to be intimate with the Holy Spirit. It's the Holy Spirit *inside* us that prepares us for His working *outside* us. I returned to New York as a girl in love. I had fallen in love with Jesus.

When we have desires that are self-inspired and world-inspired, they take over the space in us that belongs to God. When a particular desire or career possesses us, God is left out of the equation.

I see people inspired to be something, but God is saying to first *just be*. The expression *just be* means, for our purposes, to focus on becoming still and allowing the Lord to define us. One way to do this is to spend time alone with Him simply listening, as you're doing in Quiet Prayer. It's not easy to be quiet before God and sit still in His presence without asking anything or saying anything. We want to fill the air with our words. We want to let Him know we're here.

We put limits on God in many ways. We can get quite comfortable in our complaints until lack and unhappiness become a way of life that we actually begin to cling to in order to function. We need to begin to practice gratitude and decide to stop ordering God around. Begin telling yourself the things God has done for you, the joys you've experienced, and the answered prayers you've received. Love Him on His terms.

Experience the words of life in Psalm 150: "Let everything that has breath praise the LORD" (v. 6). Since everything that has breath is commanded to praise the Lord, the only scriptural excuse for not praising Him is to be out of breath!

A common misbelief is that hard work always pays off in the end. We need to learn to find rewards *within* ourselves because in life there are no guarantees. An employer of a small manufacturing company told me that no employee is indispensable because there are always other equally qualified people out there eager for a job in his company. Or how about the person who has thrust their life into a project or business that fails?

We work and we pray and we trust that God will reward us and honor His Word, which tells us, "Ask, and it will be given to you; seek, and you will find" (Matt. 7:7). When an enemy called time sneaks in, we lose heart because we think when we order God around He shouldn't take His time in answering.

Disappointment at not receiving answers to prayer when and how we want is difficult to avoid. We think we have to somehow encourage God and do something radical to impress upon Him the urgency of our request, but we don't have to bribe or beg God. He answers freely. We don't have to earn His favor; we need to stay in His presence, stay intimate with Him, and trust His will and timing, realizing that without Him our own strength and our own abilities are virtually worthless.

The Bible says, "Let the beauty of the LORD our God be upon us, and establish the work of our hands for us; yes establish the work of our hands" (Ps. 90:17).

One thing is certain as we examine dreams and our pursuits of success. What matters is how you pursue your dreams with what's inside you. It doesn't matter how clever, how smart, or how shrewd you are. If your soul is sour and your spirit bereft, you'll never know the life you were meant to have, and you won't experience lasting happiness no matter how much you achieve or accrue.

Knowing and Appreciating Your Needs

Early experiments with animals demonstrate the strong effect our needs have. Early researchers in psychological response and adjustment, Drs. George Lehner and Ella Kube, in their work *The Dynamics of Personal Adjustment*, give an example of an experiment made with an obstruction box with a mouse at one end and a piece of cheese at the other. Between the mouse and the cheese is an electrically charged grid. If the mouse is fed just prior to going into the box, he'll show only a perfunctory, mild interest in the cheese because he's not hungry. Later when he's ravenously hungry, he'll use all his efforts to get the cheese, even pushing against the electrically charged grid until he succeeds or falls over in exhaustion.[1]

Needs influence our behavior and every aspect of our lives. It's important, then, to identify what we consider needs. The psychologically hurting person usually has unrealistic and destructive needs. You may think that you need to be better looking or lose weight in order to be happy. If you believe these are needs, you'll discover down the line that your devotion to satisfying these needs will leave real needs in your life unsatisfied.

Perhaps a person believes they have a need to make a lot of money. A disproportionate drive to make money can stem from the insecure space in a person who wants to get back at the world, to spit in the eye of past deprivation and set themselves up on a high tower where being poor can't reach them. On the flip side of the drive to make money can be a genuine God-given desire to bless the Lord and do His work on earth. Money is a good thing. It's lusting after it, worrying we never have enough, misspending it, abusing what we have, hungrily wanting what others have, and not being grateful or giving that destroy us. We can destroy ourselves having too little as well as having too much when our concentration is fixed on money. God wants us to fix our minds on *Him* first.

When we lust after the wrong thing because we think we need it, the very thing we thought was so crucial can become meaningless when we get it. We easily become dissatisfied and want more.

Here's a happiness principle to practice: Discern and recognize your needs. Some needs you have are very basic, and it's important they be met. We'll talk about them in a moment. It's important to remember that needs aren't wants. Too many patients in mental hospitals and too many patients in the offices of psychologists and psychiatrists are there because of conflicted wants and needs.

There's a difference between a need and a want. A key to finding out the difference is to locate what you're telling yourself you can't live without. A client of mine in his second year of medical school told me in agony that he didn't think he could live without fulfilling his dream of becoming a doctor one day. He had been an average student in college, and now in medical school he was failing. He wanted me to help him bring up his grades and succeed in school because, he said, he *needed* to fulfill his dream. The problem was he had no interest in medicine! He was motivated not by a passion for becoming a doctor but by the fear of failing. His need was to avoid losing face. My client had never made the effort to really get to know himself and his real needs. But there's a happy ending to his story. He's now a high school gym instructor and soccer coach. He's one happy guy and doing more good for his students than he'd ever have done as an unhappy, bad physician.

Below is a list of realistic needs and unrealistic wants. You should fulfill needs, and it is realistic for you to pursue their fulfillment. The wants are not needs. You don't need them!

Realistic Needs	Unrealistic Wants
Security	To have more than others
Self-confidence	To be the greatest person alive
Friendship	Unquestioning loyalty
Respect	Adoration
Trust	Power over all situations
Love	Dependency
Skill	Brilliance, genius, to be the best
Thinking and reasoning ability	Dazzling mental abilities

Realistic Needs	Unrealistic Wants
Creativity	Masterful achievements
Freedom	Pampered pleasure
Self-discipline	License to sin
To be productive	Using busyness as avoidance behavior
To learn and grow	To be smarter and more knowledgeable than others
To give back to the world	To be applauded and heralded for your selflessness

How many of the above unrealistic wants do you recognize in your own life? What realistic needs are important to you? Write down these realistic needs in your happiness journal so you can be aware of them and not deny yourself the privilege of having them met consistently in your life. If these needs aren't recognized and met, you'll not only be frustrated but also feel you're among the disadvantaged and unlucky people in this world. Or you may be pursuing something that's not for you.

The most important need you have is the need to give back to the world. Happiness will pass you by if you don't fulfill this need. You were created to give back.

The Poverty Mind-Set

The poverty mind-set is the subtle destructive force that rears its nasty head with complaints and endless worries about money. We complain about what we don't have, what we ought to have, what we've lost, what we've ruined. We constantly worry about paying bills. We lose sleep fretting about the financial future, but it doesn't stop there. We worry about our health and the health of loved ones and about anything else that points to what's missing or what we don't have. We're focused on *lack*. All of this reflects a poverty mind-set, and it plays havoc on our emotional and physical health, and our spiritual life takes a nosedive because we aren't operating in faith. Remember that powerful force called faith? It's believing God's Word. But instead of choosing to believe in God's provision with gratitude and assurance, we sink to complaining and worrying, which lead us down the path to depression.

I found this happening in my own life. I wasn't aware of the impact that complaining and worrying about money had on me and my happiness. I had to face the truth that happiness doesn't coexist with complaining and worry. I made a serious examination of the words I spoke every day. How often did I say things like, "How will I pay for that?" or "I don't have . . ." or "I'll never be able to afford . . ."? I knew in order to be prosperous as 3 John 2 says, to prosper as my soul prospers, I'd have to make some serious attitude changes. I taught myself to stop complaining and began a concentrated, dedicated habit (building new neuro-pathways) of being grateful to and confident in the Lord. And I praised Him for what I did have. I had to put an end to a poverty mind-set that I had blindly allowed.

What a relief! What freedom! I began to fix my mind on Him instead of my needs. Quiet Prayer was a huge help in this area because being alone with the Lord without asking for anything put me in a state of worship and honoring Him for Himself, not for what He'd do for me. Once we get rid of complaining and worrying about money, we make room for real prosperity. Now I'm far more concerned about the condition of my soul and loving God than I am about money.

Value Apart from Work

As a believer in Christ, you belong to God and you're joined to Him forever. To look for self-worth without God is as hopeless as hunting for orchids in wintry Montana. Jesus is Lord of your needs. Will you accept that reality right now before going any further? Free yourself now. I like this quotation by Mother Teresa: "We must free ourselves to be filled by God."[2]

I overheard a teenager telling her friends in the hallway of a church where I was speaking, "To not accept Jesus as my Lord would be sheer craziness." Don't be intimidated by the culture or intellect of our age. There's no need big enough to intimidate God!

When our ideals and standards are unrealistically demanding, we always have the feeling our lives aren't being lived as well as they could be. We're prey to the "musts" and "shoulds" and "ought tos" of life.

Achievement is one measure of fulfillment, and to the person with high goals, it becomes a major measure of fulfillment. This is unrealistic. They feel achievement gives them the right to feel fulfilled. The person then sets goals that are over-demanding and require extremely rigorous dedication—something a happy person knows better than to do.

Happiness isn't an end in itself; it's a beginning. The happiness I'm talking about in this book is happiness that burns from within. It's inextinguishable. Happy people don't fall prey to proving themselves. Happy people have much more to give the world because they have no demands on the world to fulfill their needs. Happy people don't harbor unmet expectations.

One of the preachers I interviewed told me of his enormous craving to be needed when he was young in the ministry. His need to be needed dominated his life. It took failure and disgrace to cure him, he said. "It used to be I could concentrate on nothing else but building my ministry. I was in love with the idea of being the one with the answers, the one who brought help and healing to people, and having a *big* church. I was the man. I was the one who needed to be needed." He said ministry could be summed up in three words: me, me, and me. He didn't know he orchestrated his own demise by failing to understand that unless God builds the house, it's built in vain (Ps. 127:1). We can't play God.

Broken and wounded after being booted out of the church he had worked so hard to build, he began to rebuild himself. At the root of overachieving is the deadly sin of pride. It took over ten years for this pastor to rebuild his life and ministry, which now is helping thousands of people rebuild their lives. He learned from his failure. He learned to focus on God's work, not his. And now his failure has been turned to good.

The housewife, the minister, the woman back in the workforce, the executive—none of them can be all things to all people. We can't be all things to ourselves, and we can't be all things to God. Often the person with high expectations will think of themselves as a person chosen and set apart to accomplish something so special and unique that God could choose only them to do it. This person believes they are a really special person God can't do without.

Unhappily, such misbeliefs create pressure to achieve and succeed, and unhappiness is their constant companion.

Answer the following questions:

1. Do you feel guilty when you take time off from work?
2. Do you feel you overextend yourself?
3. Do you consider yourself a competitive person?
4. When you do a good job, do you expect and demand recognition for it?
5. Are you impatient with delays or interruptions?

If you answered yes to any of the questions above, you're probably under a lot of daily pressure. It's time to take a good look at yourself, your goals, and your motives for your work and personal life. It's time to practice letting go.

It's not a bad thing to want to do well and succeed. Far from it. But in our zeal to perform our lives well, we can go beyond the limits of God's leading.

What we do and have aren't proof of our personal value. Jesus did not die on the cross for you so that you would have to earn your personal value. You are a winner because you simply are. Stress-prone people have very little good to offer the world because their main focus is themselves.

Tell yourself you're a new person in Christ. All the old things are long gone. Memorize this Scripture passage:

> Therefore if any person is [engrafted] in Christ (the Messiah) he is a new creation (a new creature altogether); the old [previous moral and spiritual condition] has passed away. Behold, the fresh and new has come! (2 Cor. 5:17 AMP)

Remind yourself of Psalm 91:1 and your true dwelling place, your holy habitation for withdrawing into God's presence. It is a covering and the secret place of the Most High. Make the words personal. I'm covered. I dwell in the secret place of the Most High, and I live under the glorious shadow of the Almighty. The Amplified version says, "He who dwells in the secret place of the Most High shall remain stable and fixed under the shadow of the Almighty [Whose power no foe can withstand]." The Message says, "You who sit down in the High God's presence, spend the night in Shaddai's shadow, say this: 'GOD, you're my refuge!'"

The Lord knows you need meaningful work. He knows your heart. He wants you to know true and lasting happiness, and *so you will.*

Now is a good time to enter your five-minute Quiet Prayer before you go on to the next chapter. If you can learn to practice stilling your mind in the quietness of the presence of God as I'm suggesting, you'll soon be amazed at the difference in your daily life.

Faulty Escapes

When I met with Kathy on a sunny Tuesday afternoon, she was vibrant and talkative. She was eager to give me an account of how well her life was going. As she went on, I listened with the feeling that something was amiss. Then she said, "Oh, by the way, I have to go into the hospital on Thursday for a biopsy. My doctor is concerned about a lump."

So that was it.

"The doctor says it's routine. They're very thorough, you know." She told me this while smiling and fidgeting with the handle of her purse. As a therapist and life coach, I've learned that the things people tell me last are usually the things most important to them. "Kathy," I said, "do you want me to go with you?"

Suddenly her face lost the glossy, carefree look. "I'm not worried, of course! I know God will be with me, but it'll be comforting to know you'll be there too."

She didn't want me to think she was the least bit nervous. She denied that there could be anything upsetting about the possibility of something being wrong with her body. But her denial of her anxiety and fear could actually cause her *more* fear and anxiety in the long run. A happiness skill is learning to face our fears head-on.

The Way of Escape

Nobody enjoys being stressed-out or anxious. We want to be happy people, so when we're faced with anxiety-arousing situations, if we can't deal with our feelings, we come up with ways to escape them. Here are the four main ways we try to escape and mask our fears and anxieties:

1. Deny them. (I do not feel what I feel.)
2. Avoid them. (I feel what I feel, but I'll avoid facing what I feel. I'll think about that tomorrow.)
3. Rationalize them. (Everything is really okay because we're all human and nobody's perfect.)
4. Narcotize them. (Doing drugs, drinking, sleeping, excessive TV watching, overeating.)

Denial

Denial is a powerful defense against facing our fears and negative feelings. My friend Kathy didn't want to face her fears of what she called the C word, so she denied her feelings and covered them with a shaky belief that all would turn out rosy.

Denial is an attempt to disavow the existence of unpleasant reality. But when we deny our negative feelings, we open ourselves up to unmanageable inner turmoil. If you perceive something to be painful or threatening, denying the feeling will only increase a sense of uncertainty and instability.

Denial is a means of coping that denies what we feel. The truth of a situation is too painful to face, so we deny its relevance or even its existence. Scarlett O'Hara, in the book and movie *Gone with the Wind*, gives us a good illustration of denial when her world falls apart and she says, "I won't think about that today. I'll think about it tomorrow."

Jeanne tells me that Joe, her on-again-off-again boyfriend, wants her to loan him money to start a new business. She tells me this with a big, cheesy smile. "Of course he'll pay me back."

"Has he paid you back all the money he's already borrowed from you?" I innocently ask.

"Well, yes, I mean—well, no, not exactly all of it."

I pause. "How much of what he already owes you has he actually paid back?"

She's edgy now. "Oh heavens, I haven't really kept track. I don't know. He means well."

Another pause. "Explain what you mean by 'means well.'"

"Really, Marie. He totally *intends* to pay it all back." The cheesy smile fades.

I wonder who she's talking to, who she's trying to convince. On she talks. "Joe needs this loan for a really great business opportunity that he's come up with. He stands to make a lot of money, and then he says he'll pay me back with interest!"

Do you see denial here? Jeanne can't, or won't, face the truth that Joe is taking her for a ride. She's handed over thousands of dollars, none of which he's made the slightest effort to pay back. The person in denial will make excuses for their denial with statements like those Jeanne made.

The alcoholic and drug addict are almost always in some state of denial. "No, not me! I don't have a problem! I can stop any time!" "I don't drink too much!" "I can handle the drugs. I'm not addicted!" The alcoholic and the addict lie to themselves and deny the significance of the endless problems associated with drinking or drugging. The loss of jobs, bad relationships, poor health, and DUIs are all due to some outside circumstance, rotten luck, stupid laws, or an injustice done to them.

Here are some triggers to watch for with denial:

- staying in a bad relationship while denying its destructiveness
- refusing to admit personal limitations
- refusing to acknowledge negative and harmful habits
- spending money you don't have and getting into debt you can't pay back
- demanding others be what you want them to be instead of appreciating them for who they are
- attempting to be something you aren't
- blaming others for your personal problems
- acting superior to others
- behaving in any way that's false or misleading
- lying

Avoidance

We engage in avoidance behavior when we're willing to talk about anything except our fears. Avoidance is different from denial in that denial says, "Who me? I don't have a problem," while avoidance says, "Okay, I have a problem, but it's my own business. I'll put it on the back burner for now." (Shades of Scarlett O'Hara here.) Avoidance talk always includes, "Let's just see what happens," or the abominable snowman of expressions, "Whatever."

The person who realizes there's a problem avoids doing something about it by telling themselves that their problems are private. No need to bring them out in the open, and no need to do something about them now. "Everyone has their vices." The person in avoidance doesn't want anyone to pry into their life to make them take a good look at themselves and what they fear.

Rationalization

When we rationalize, we make excuses for our bad behavior or our problems. The alcoholic says, "I have a good reason to drink.

If you were in my shoes, you'd drink too." Failure is something we commonly rationalize. We rationalize our failures rather than learn from them. In failed relationships, we rationalize that the fault wasn't ours—we had good reasons for our actions. "We broke up because I'd had it with their problems." Physical and verbal abuse are always accompanied by rationalization. "She deserved it." "He asked for it!" "I can't help it!" "My problems are not my fault, so I don't have to deal with them!" "It's their fault." As long as we can blame someone or something else, we don't have to be responsible for our behavior.

Narcotizing

We narcotize ourselves against fear and anxiety in a number of ways, such as oversleeping, excessive TV watching, shopping, overeating, talking on the telephone—in other words, escape behaviors that become addictive. Mind-altering drugs aren't just found on the street and back alleys of a nonbelieving world. Many Christians turn to mind-numbing substances in the form of alcohol and pills as a means of relaxation, relief, and escape. These can turn into serious addictions.

Misbeliefs Associated with Faulty Escapes

Here are some telltale misbeliefs associated with denial, avoidance, rationalization, and the use of narcotics as unhealthy ways to escape fear and anxiety:

- I don't want to talk about it. It's not important.
- Not me. I don't have problems or fears.
- My problems aren't that bad.
- I have good reasons for my problems, so I don't have to deal with them.

- I can prove that my problems are not my fault, so I don't have to deal with them.
- Others are worse off than I am, and that proves my problems aren't serious.
- I'll pretend to be who others want me to be so they don't know the real me.
- I'll only admit that I have problems if someone agrees to solve them for me.
- I feel good, so that means there's nothing wrong with me.
- Since nothing works, I don't have to try.
- I have the right to destroy myself, and no one has the right to stop me.

To Fear or Not to Fear

From the day we can walk, we're taught to be brave little soldiers, especially little boys. "Big boys don't cry." "Be a man." "Think like a hero." We're taught we're sissies if we're afraid. Little girls are taught it's not pretty to cry. Along with the message that fear is bad, we're also taught to be terrified. "Don't go in the street. You'll get hit by a car and die!" "Don't touch that!" "You'll poke your eye out!" "Don't eat that! You'll get sick!" So many things to be afraid of. I remember being afraid to play with a big girl my age in kindergarten because I heard my dad say if she sat on me she could crush me to death.

Mixed messages. We learn that to be afraid is bad, but we also learn that there are countless things to be terrified of!

Fear can be a good thing when it causes us to act. God created our brains to *act* on fear, not deny it. It's late and the children aren't home yet, so we get on the phone to find out where they are and if they're safe. A tornado is heading our way, so we get to a place of protection.

What about the things that cause fear that we can't do something about, like the company's downsizing, or the airplane we're on that starts flipping around in the air like a kite, or the guy in a mask who enters the bank with a gun?

Here's where the inner you jumps in and takes over. Here's where your inner spiritual work reveals the real you. I'm suggesting you continue to deepen your Quiet Prayer moments in order to build your inner strength and enliven yourself in the power of the Holy Spirit for the times when you face the most difficult and painful situations. Permit your fearful words and thoughts to drop into the Lord's hands throughout the day. Perfect love casts out fear, and you, my friend, are perfectly loved.

If you follow my suggestions for Quiet Prayer in this book, you'll discover a new mind-set strengthening you when you're faced with a tough or frightening situation. You might possibly hear in the back of your mind, "Be still, and know that I am God" (Ps. 46:10), and sense peace and confidence coming over you. With the wonder of who He is within you, very gently open your soul to His leading.

Dealing with Fear

Fear is a happiness-robbing emotion, and trying to escape fear is an unhealthy response. The good news is there are tools you can use to deal with fear so you can be happy in an unhappy world. The world around you may be unhappy and confused, but not you.

The first step in neutralizing fear is to recognize and admit your feelings. "You shall know the truth, and the truth shall make you free" (John 8:32). Allow the truth to jostle around inside you right now. Open the eyes of your mind.

The second step is to practice inner stillness. Don't rush this. Stay here. It doesn't matter how much noise is going on around you. Go inside to that secret place and allow your thoughts to quiet down.

The third step is to call upon the verses you've memorized. Here are some verses from God's arsenal of protection and help in time of need:

- "I can do all things through Christ who strengthens me" (Phil. 4:13).
- "You are of God . . . and have overcome . . . because He who is in you is greater than he who is in the world" (1 John 4:4).
- "You are complete in Him, who is the head of all principality and power" (Col. 2:10).
- "There is no fear in love; but perfect love casts out fear" (1 John 4:18).
- "He who dwells in the secret place of the Most High shall abide under the shadow of the Almighty" (Ps. 91:1).
- "For God has not given us a spirit of fear, but of power and of love and of a sound mind" (2 Tim. 1:7).

Don't be shy about repeating a verse. Repeat one verse all day long if you have to. I love the Chaplet of Divine Mercy in which for a half hour or so the congregation is led in singing the words, "For the sake of His sorrowful passion, have mercy on us and on the whole world." Not being Catholic, I was unaware the first time I heard this that it was the first day of the Divine Mercy Novena initiated by St. Faustina. (A novena is a series of prayers said for nine days straight.) I didn't know there were many ways to pray this novena and more than one musical adaptation. I bought a CD, and every time I pray and sing along with the CD, I begin to weep about five minutes into it.

When you repeat the words of a prayer, a psalm, or a Scripture passage over and over again, they explode in you and around you in a shower of revelation. I simply can't take part in the Chaplet of Divine Mercy without crying. As I sing the words, I go to the cross, I go to the magnificence of God's forgiveness, I go to the stunning gift of life He gives us by indwelling us. Don't be afraid to repeat Scripture or words of glorious faith. When your heart is open, the repetition can be something glorious.

You might ask if crying is a happy thing to do. I have to answer yes, because everything that brings me to a more deeply centered place in Christ leads to happiness.

Sometimes we can be afraid of something and not realize it. A good example is harboring a dread of saying the wrong thing or of coming across badly. This fear, if never dealt with, ferments inside the soul and gets confused with shyness. But shyness is often an excuse. It may be that you're not shy, but rather that you're full of yourself.

Being oblivious to your fears brings on happiness robbers such as suspicion, distrust, and diffidence that if unchecked can take over your life. You'll be suspicious. You won't trust people. You'll shrink into yourself. Only by facing our fears can we know what it is to be brave.

The Daredevil Mentality

We all know someone we think of as a daredevil. That's the person who seems to look for and thrive on danger. It's not that they have no fear. It's that some people deny their fear by doing outrageously frightening acts. To boast, "Nothing scares me" can signal a denial of fear. They may be very much afraid, and to compensate for that fear, to squash it down, they compromise their safety. To that person, fear or being afraid is a negative thing. The daredevil often isn't in touch with their fears, and they often have no idea that their brave acts are compensating for an abhorrence for weakness and a fear of being weak or afraid.

The true hero admits their weaknesses and their fear and works through them. There are so many heroes I could name, such as firefighters, like my brother, who put their lives on the line each time they climb into a uniform, and our military men and women who dare to face danger in spite of their apprehensions and fears. Notice I said *in spite of* their fears, not by denying their fears.

Every human being on the planet experiences fear. It's what we do with our fear that shapes us. All of our emotions are important. To deny ourselves the right to experience fear is denying ourselves the right to be human. Trying to escape fear will cause us to live our lives in one long postponement with only glimpses of happiness.

Close your eyes and pause for a few minutes of Quiet Prayer as you let go of your fears and anxiety before we go on to the next chapter, where I'll talk more about fear and how to get rid of its grip.

The Fears That Kill You

The Fear of Being Alone

There was a time I thought the fear of being alone was a problem that pertained mostly to women. Not true. I have found that men actually fear being alone more than women do.

The fear of being alone and denying the fear of being alone both produce negative behaviors. If you're afraid of being alone, you'll fill up your life with countless trivial activities and meaningless relationships. And you'll make some serious mistakes. Denying the fear of being alone can produce great conflict within you if you're an outgoing person because you've convinced yourself that you love people (when actually you're afraid of losing people). You'll also make mistakes you'll regret.

One of my clients tells herself, when she starts feeling lonely, "Hey, I'm not alone. I've got me!" I like that.

You're never alone. You've got you.

The person who's afraid to be alone and denies that fear can become incredibly self-engrossed. They will pity themselves and continue to pity themselves even when things are going well and their prayers are answered.

Henri Nouwen wrote, "As long as we approach another person from our loneliness, no mature human relationship can develop. Clinging to one another in loneliness is suffocating and eventually becomes destructive. For love to be possible we need the courage to create space between us and to trust that this space allows us to dance together."[1]

Being alone is actually a good thing. Imagine if Beethoven's Ninth Symphony had been written by a committee. Can you imagine Shakespeare's *King Lear* or *Hamlet* as a collective effort? Could Michelangelo's *Pieta* have been sculpted as magnificently if it had been done by a battalion of art students with chisels?

It's time we faced ourselves with joyful appreciation. For better or worse, you must play your own little instrument in the orchestra of life. And with God in you as your Conductor, you make the most beautiful sound in the world. The trick is to hear it for yourself.

Being alone doesn't mean we're rejected or alienated. It means we're with ourselves. And we're with God. You don't need people to be fulfilled. You need a relationship with God.

A divorced man in our church told me how he longed to find the right woman, and he said he looked at single women wondering, "Is she the one?" He told himself continually that he was lonely and "it is not good that man should be alone" (Gen. 2:18). He bitterly envied happy-appearing married couples and daydreamed of a woman who would love him unconditionally and would completely fulfill his every need, a fiction he lived with daily. He got to the point that when Ms. All-Wrong showed up and showered him with false attention, he bought it. He tied himself up in an ungodly relationship, telling himself at least he wasn't alone. Two years and some deep scars later, she left him for someone else, and he was again alone and broken.

The fear of being alone is a happiness thief. And latching on to another person to escape the fear of being alone is not a solution to loneliness. Signs to recognize include the following:

- spending hours on the telephone yakking about your problems instead of seeking real help from God
- being addicted to social media
- partying and pursuing a jam-packed social life
- going to any length, even if it is against your principles, for favor
- spending money foolishly and getting into debt
- becoming clingy and overly possessive
- if single, wasting time dating the wrong person who spiritually robs you (and God help you if you marry the person)

I could go on with the list. All of these behaviors are reflections of spiritual hunger. The fear of being alone is life-swallowing. It feeds ungodliness and neurotic self-centeredness bordering on narcissism.

Loneliness as a Gift

The Holy Spirit within you tells you you're never alone because He's with you always. Set yourself apart for time each day to meditate on His presence. Begin by admitting you're afraid to be alone. There is no crime in being afraid to be alone. Once you've admitted your fear, rest and let go. Continue to practice letting go and sinking your heart deeper and deeper into your relationship with God. Give yourself permission to begin to enjoy Him as He deserves to be enjoyed.

I know what it's like to be lonely, but I've learned there's a difference between disliking the feeling of loneliness and being afraid of it. I've taught myself some skills to deal with feelings of loneliness that work for me, and the first one I pull out of my happiness tool kit is to accept loneliness as a gift. Loneliness always represents human desires, but they can be skewed. (I dated guys I had nothing in common with just to be dating someone because if you're single and don't date, there must be something wrong with you, right?)

There came a moment in my life when I accepted the feeling of loneliness as a blessed gift and not a social disease needing a cure. I read the writings of great Christians such as St. John of the Cross (1542–91), who speaks so passionately about the "dark hour of the soul" and aching for his silent God. He writes, "Stricken by love, I lost myself, and was found."[2]

The Polish saint Sister Faustina (1905–38) wrote in her diary, "How fleeting all earthly things are, and everything that appears great disappears like smoke, and does not give the soul freedom, but weariness. Happy the soul that understands these things and with only one foot touches the earth."[3]

American-born Maria Etter Woodworth (1844–1924) lost five children before she embarked on a life serving God and preaching. She knew about grief and loneliness. She was misunderstood, rejected, and arrested for conducting healings in her meetings. She was kicked out of town more than once for being a woman preacher. She lost two husbands and suffered much illness in her life, and here is what she said: "Heaven is full of power and energy. When we have an experience with heaven, power is what is flowing through us. You can't put your finger in a socket and remain still. How much more should we be full of energy when we touch God?"[4]

My friend Mario says we can never be lonely when we have true love. I like that. Love is the key, the mystical key, to the end of loneliness. Loving God is a full-hearted endeavor, not something we tinker with when the mood moves us. Loving God is a choice, and it's joyous. It produces a thrilling, wondrous relationship. To believe that people, friendships, lovers, activities, work, or recreation will eliminate loneliness is a mistake leading to massive disappointment.

The Gospel of Peace

The gospel lives in you, like the Light lives in you. The angels proclaimed the gospel with, "On earth peace, goodwill toward men!" (Luke 2:14), and Jesus said, "Peace to you" before He said, "As the Father has sent Me, I also send you" (John 20:21). Peace comes first, and when Jesus speaks of peace, He means peace within you, deep and true.

You can always tell a person who lives inside the gospel of peace by the peace that emanates from their presence. A speaker can get up on a platform and preach a powerful sermon but not have peace. I know this to be true because I've been there. I've preached my heart out, but in the deepest core of me, there wasn't the peace Jesus spoke of when He said, "My peace I give to you; not as the world gives. . . . Let not your heart be troubled, neither let it be afraid" (John 14:27). If I'd been in the boat on the Sea of Galilee when the storm hit, I'd have panicked just like His disciples. I'd have been the first one to start bailing water with my bare hands and crying for my life.

I'm learning it's possible to be a high-energy person and peaceful at the same time. I've learned, and I continue to learn day by day, to lean into the space of my spirit and be at peace in all situations. I'm learning what it means to just *be*. It takes work on my part to quiet a racing mind, not to mention silencing a quick temper. Quiet Prayer is a real spiritual and mental workout for me because in reality my Gethsemane would be an empty gym. Energy and agitation can't occupy the same area of space at the same time. I choose to turn my natural energy to God and shut tight the gates to agitation.

A man took his little girl to buy an ice-cream cone. A drunk came up behind them and shoved the man against the wall to get through the door first. The man not only allowed himself to be pushed but also graciously opened the door for the drunk to pass through before him. A woman watching the scene said, "Are you going to let that bum get away with that?" The man simply smiled and answered, "I can afford to let him go first."

Those are words that touch the heart of God. The man had peace in his heart *before* the drunk guy bullied and shoved him.

The man didn't have to stop and pray or think about what to do. Peace showed him what to do. He stood back and allowed the bully to go first. Who can you let go first? What can you let go of? Peace that passes understanding can't be faked. And if you have peace, you won't be fearful. Real peace is the very soul of happiness.

Joan of Arc (1413–31), a young French peasant girl, heard from God and out of love for God stood before the entire civilized world as she knew it and fearlessly proclaimed what she had heard. She had heard from heaven that she was to liberate France from the English, and at seventeen, the young, uneducated, untrained peasant girl led an army of mighty trained soldiers to win a battle at Orleans. After accepting the surrender of Troyes, she and her army escorted Charles VII to Rheims for his coronation in 1429.

Joan was later captured and handed over to the English to be tried for witchcraft. She proclaimed, "I would rather die than do something which I know to be a sin, or to be against God's will." She was tried by a group of clergy who had to be coerced into finding her guilty of witchcraft, and she died a horrible death by being burned alive at the stake. They had to burn her three times because her heart and other organs refused to burn. She said before she died, "One life is all we have and we live it as we believe in living it. But to sacrifice what you are and to live without belief, that is a fate more terrible than dying."[5] She is loved and treasured across the globe to this day, the brave teenager whose life in Christ was built on the power of love, which is so much greater than fear.

The Fear of Being Worthless

To be happy and *stay* happy in an unhappy world, you must consider yourself in the light of who you are. The misbelief that a person is not precious or valuable if they make mistakes, do something stupid, don't look good, fail, procrastinate, behave poorly, take a moral tumble, ruin a good thing, lose the game for the team—fill in the blank—is death! These are lies to run for your life from. When you avoid confrontation with your negative, self-pitying, judgmental, nonproductive self-talk, it doesn't matter how much beauty or goodness you encounter. Your life won't be a happy one.

Charles S. Carver and Ronald J. Ganellen of the University of Florida at Gainesville wrote an article for the *Journal of Abnormal Psychology* on why people get depressed.[6] They devised a test to prove three attitudes that may lead to depression:

1. trying to meet impossible standards
2. being too harsh on oneself in instances of failure
3. overgeneralizing, when one allows individual failures to make them feel worthless

Carver and Ganellen determined through their studies that over-generalizing was the strongest attitude on their depression index.

Feelings of worthlessness must be approached and examined head-on. Such fears keep us in jobs we hate and relationships that are miserable. We never see the world and ourselves as God intended.

If you harbor feelings of not being worth much and you deny these feelings, you probably lean toward overachieving. Your achievements might be exactly the same as those of a person who has a lot of self-confidence, but the difference is you don't believe what you're doing is worthwhile. And no matter how well you do something, how many achievements and accolades you stack up for yourself, if you have unacknowledged or untended fears rumbling around, you'll never fully enjoy God's blessings that are yours.

God is whispering encouragement in your ear. He's breathing His love into your heart and kissing away your fears and your self-doubts. "I love you with an eternal, forever love," He is telling you. "I created you perfectly and I delight in you. It's with loving-kindness I draw you to Myself so you can see yourself as I see you" (see Jer. 31:3).

Running with the Wind

My good friends Lois and Gunter Hofmann circumnavigated the world for eight years in their forty-three-foot custom-built Catana catamaran called *Pacific Bliss*. They tell of a harrowing, life-threatening experience in the Colombian basin when they were heading for W. Gallinas Point, the northernmost cape in South America. They had skirted the peninsula of Guajira, and suddenly the wind increased from force 8 to force 9. (Force 8 equals a gale.) The crests of the waves crashed all around them. Within hours, the wind speed increased to fifty-plus knots, a force 10. The waves were as high as four-story buildings. Force 12 is a deadly hurricane. There was little hope for them to survive such a storm. Lois explained to me that when a storm hits while you are at sea in a catamaran, you don't fight it. You have to run with it. If you fight each passing wave, resist each undertow, confront each swell, and battle against the raging current, the boat will get tossed about and possibly destroyed. "We had no choice but to run with the wind," she said. At last when the wind decreased to a force 8, they managed to keep from capsizing, and with the wind lashing at their port side, they finally reached Cartagena Bay safely with little damage done to their boat. (Read the entire story in Lois's book *Maiden Voyage*,[7] the first of the trilogy of their sailing adventures.)

In life, you're going to hit force 12 winds. Wild, unpredictable, screeching storms will hit as you journey along on your sea of life. It's a given. But you have a choice. You can fight against the crashing waves in a furious assault against the beast of the sea, or you can coil into a fetal position in fear of death. Or you can take the advice of experienced life sailors and "run with the wind."

If you turn to God for help only in times of peril, the risk you take every day is bigger than any storm out there. You're unprepared! Lois and Gunter were prepared for the nightmare they faced out on the ocean. As terrifying as the experience was, they didn't panic.

Wise decisions aren't made in a panic. We bring intimacy with God into the crowded, unpredictable ocean of life with our schedules and our work, but it's in the quiet hours alone with Him that He prepares us for the wild and furious storms that are bound to hit.

The Fear of Happiness

If you've been wounded in the past by betrayal, as I talked about in chapter 5, or if you've lost something or someone that made you happy, a residue of fear could still fester in you, telling you to beware of being happy because you'll surely lose it.

Brandon is thirty-seven years old and has held more jobs than he can count. He was recently fired from his latest job, and three weeks before that, his girlfriend called it quits and left him. Each time Brandon loses a job and/or a girlfriend, he can't figure out what went wrong. Clearly, he doesn't think he's to blame. When he tries to come up with answers, they're excuses. Brandon is afraid of happiness. He's fond of saying nothing lasts forever.

He reminds me of the circus lion in the play *Don Quixote* who longed to be free from his cage, out in the open air. One day the cage was accidentally left open, and the lion leapt out to freedom. Once free, the reality of all that freedom suddenly hit him, and terrified, he turned and raced back into the cage. Sometimes it's more comfortable to be miserable. It's more familiar.

The Greek word *anhedonia* means "the diminished ability to experience satisfaction and pleasure." For the person who's afraid to be truly happy because of the fear of losing it or what it will cost, *anhedonia* can become a permanent way of life.

The responsibility for staying happy is too much for some of us. It's downright frightening and keeps us in a state of being unable to experience real satisfaction or pleasure.

One of the traits of the fear of happiness is self-denigration. If you're afraid to be happy, you'll always find fault with yourself no matter how much you achieve or how much you do. You'll discount your kind deeds as nothing. You'll undermine your faith and your strength of character. When you're afraid to be happy, it's easier to be the bad guy, the curmudgeon, the troublemaker.

Here's an exercise for you to complete in your happiness journal:

1. List some fears, such as the fear of someone finding out your secrets. Give these to Jesus, who said His burden is light (Matt. 11:30).
2. Give yourself the right to your feelings and write them down, both negative and positive.
3. Write down two rationalizations you want to change forever.
4. Write a prayer to Jesus asking Him to help you handle negative feelings and create something new and beautiful out of them.

Your Feelings Aren't Who You Are

Perhaps you respond to pleasure and happiness intellectually rather than emotionally, but you have the right to your good feelings *and* your bad feelings.

Parents who tell their children, "Stop crying this minute!" or "Stop acting so droopy" teach their children that negative feelings are bad. People take this misbelief into adulthood and experience shame, guilt, doubt, worry, and so on because not all their feelings are good or nice.

As Christians, we want to be holy before the Lord, and we mistake this to mean that we are to eradicate anything about us that's not ideal. When we try to do this, we incur guilt and shame because we're imperfect mortals and sinners saved by grace.

Imagine yourself staying happy without a shred of guilt, sadness, or fear for several days in a row. Imagine yourself being the one who pulls the strings for your happiness levels. You're the one in control. Let go of the guilt, let go of the shame, and be at peace with who you are in Christ right now. Your feelings don't identify who you are. Your faith does.

You can smooth the surface of metal with tools, but if you want to change its shape, it must go through the fiery forge to be new from the inside out. Quiet Prayer will help you change from the inside out.

Too much of our Christian life is lived on the surface, with Christ "out there" as our help in time of need instead of within us. We pray, "Help me" as though we're all alone. In you, in the heart of you, the core essence of you, God has made a home for Himself. He's alive inside you. In the secret place within, God lives, and guess what—He's *happy* to be in you.

Imagine telling yourself you can handle happiness. How does that feel? What does it feel like to be completely fearless? Talk to Jesus about this feeling. Write it in your happiness journal. Continue with a five-minute Quiet Prayer with the Author and Sustainer of lasting happiness. Sit in an upright position, fully aware. Gently close your eyes and still your mind. Imagine yourself sitting with Jesus right beside you or before you—just you and Him. Let everything go except the knowledge of being with Him as He offers you the gift of happiness.

Beloved

You were loved long before you were wounded. Before your parents, teachers, spouses, children, and friends loved or wounded you, you were loved by the Lover of your soul, Jesus.

That's the truth.

Claim Him. Own Him.

There's a soft, gentle voice that speaks in the silence and solitude of your heart, wanting to be heard. Jesus calls you His beloved.

This is your core truth.

He knows you're under pressure to prove your worth, to do something relevant, something spectacular, to earn approval and attention. He understands. He knows how you've turned to people, things, and events to fill your life. He sees your spiritual longing, and He's here now. His arms are out to you, and He's eager to fold you into His joy. He's here to give your life purpose and meaning, for you are chosen and treasured as His beloved one. Let Him show you the sweet path of lasting happiness.

Imagine the Lord speaking to you now. Imagine Him whispering in your ear:

I have called you by name from the very beginning.
You are Mine and I am yours.
    You are My beloved; My favor rests on you.
I knitted you together in your mother's womb.
    I carved you in the palms of My hands,
and I hide you in the shadow of My embrace.
    I look at you with infinite tenderness and care
more intimate than that of a mother for her child.
    I have counted every hair on your head,
and I guide your steps. Wherever you go,
    I go with you, and wherever you rest,
I keep watch. I will give you food that will satisfy
    your hunger and drink that will quench
all your thirst. I will not hide My face from you.
    Know Me as your own as I know you as My own.
You belong to Me. I am your father, your mother,
    your brother, your sister, your lover, and your spouse.
We are one.[1]

As long as being the beloved of God remains in your mind simply as a beautiful thought or a sweet idea, it'll stay in your mind as information only, like a note posted on Facebook. Your mind is not your spirit. God is Spirit, so when He speaks to you, it's Spirit to spirit. Your mind can hold a thought, but your spirit holds life. What's required from you to live as the beloved of God in your daily life is that you close the gap between your mind and your spirit. Think about what you're absorbing into your spirit from the Spirit of God. The life of the Spirit of God in you has everything to do with the way you think, talk, and act in your daily life and what you think about and do from hour to hour.

I've given students the assignment to take out their calendars and day planners and write out what they plan to *think* about for the next two days. This is a shocking concept, and I'm usually met with confused expressions, like I must be kidding. Then I tell them that the thoughts they choose must be truths from God's heart, not something like, "I'll think about how cute Jim or Jana is" or "I'll think about what I'll eat for dinner." I give them an example of my own: "This is the day the Lord has made. I will rejoice and be glad in it."

Hands go up. "What about other thoughts?" they want to know. "What if I think about how the Chargers are doing?" "What if I get angry about something?"

I explain that this exercise is about planning *specific* thoughts to have during the day; they won't be our *only* thoughts. The average person thinks from fifty thousand to seventy thousand thoughts per day, which averages out to about thirty-five to forty-eight thoughts per minute. Most people haven't begun to tap into this monumentally enormous reservoir of influence.

If you can plan specific thoughts to think for one day at a time, you'll amaze yourself. I designed this exercise to help us learn to tether the wildness of our thought life and to bring *focus* and *purpose* into our lives as God's beloved. As you may recall, two things cannot occupy the same area of space at the same time. So you can't have negative and positive thoughts occupying your brain at the same time!

Four Aspects of the Beloved

Let's look at four aspects of being the beloved of God.

1. Chosen
2. Blessed
3. Broken
4. Possessed

Chosen

As a child of God, you are chosen. "You did not choose Me, but I chose you," Jesus said (John 15:16). And He chose you for a definite purpose that the world can't duplicate. "I chose you out of the world!" (John 15:19). "Many are called (invited and summoned) but few are chosen" (Matt. 22:14 AMP). The word *chosen* is *eklektos* in the Greek, which means choice, select, the best of its class, excellent, preeminent, and applied to certain individual Christians. Your uniqueness has been noticed in heaven. God has observed you, and He has expressed a desire to come closer to you. God has seen you from every corner of eternity, long before you were born and became a part of history. When you choose Him back, He pours Himself into you for a relationship unparalleled on earth.

In the midst of painful reality, we have to dare to claim the truth that we are God's chosen even when our world ignores or mistreats us. We no longer are caught in the indifferent net of a world that accepts or rejects according to its own agendas and control. It's a lifelong work because the world persists in its efforts to pull us into the darkness of self-doubt, depression, low self-esteem—or worse, pride and empty vaunting.

Long before any human being saw you or touched you, God saw you. Long before you heard a human voice, God was speaking to you. Hold on to your chosenness. Hold on tight. Here are some guidelines to help you:

1. Keep unmasking the temptations that surround you for what they are—manipulating, controlling, and in the long run destructive.

2. Every time you feel hurt, offended, or rejected, dare to proclaim, "These feelings, strong as they may be, are not the truth about me. I reject them. The truth, even if I can't see it right now, is that I am a chosen child of God, precious in God's eyes, called beloved from all eternity, and held safe in His embrace!"

3. Stay close to people who speak the truth and places where the truth is spoken and where you're reminded of your deepest identity as a chosen child of God.

4. Celebrate your chosenness. Celebrate continually. This means thanking God for having chosen you and thanking all those who remind you of your chosenness. Gratitude is the most fruitful way of freeing yourself from yourself.

Blessed

In Latin, the word *bless* is *benedicere*, from which we get our word *benediction*. It literally means "speaking well" or saying good things about someone. But it's more than that. Deuteronomy 28:8 says, "The LORD will command *the* blessing on you in your storehouses and in all to which you set your hand, and He will bless you in the land which the LORD your God is giving you" (emphasis added). When God blesses us with the force and power of His blessing, the other blessings of life follow. Proverbs 10:22 says, "The blessing of the LORD makes one rich, and He adds no sorrow with it."

To give someone a blessing is the most significant affirmation we can offer. It's more than a word of praise or appreciation; it's more than pointing out someone's talents or good deeds. It's putting someone in the light of love. To give a blessing is to affirm, to say yes to God's love for that person. God spoke His blessing on His people by saying, "Blessing I will bless you" (Gen. 22:17), and we tap into this towering, inclusive blessing to release it to others, obeying His Word, which says, "And you shall be a blessing" (Gen. 12:2). When you bless another person, you're speaking spiritual prosperity to their spirit, soul, and body.

How can you bless another person if you don't know how to be blessed? Go back to my suggestion earlier in this chapter and begin to plan your thoughts for the day. Choose your thoughts carefully. See and experience your blessedness in an unambiguous way. Be in touch with your own blessedness, and meditate on what it means to be blessed by God. Wear your blessings and the promises of God as an impenetrable shield.

Broken

"Out of brokenness beauty is born," claims Mickey O'Neill McGrath, whose artistic expressions illustrate the joy and exuberance of faith in Christ.[2]

Julian of Norwich (1342–1420) wrote the oldest book in English by a woman, called *Revelations of Divine Love*, a timeless work that has remained century after century a powerful source of contemporary spirituality. In it, she tells of receiving a vision of a little thing, the size of a hazelnut in the palm of her hand. She wondered what it was and heard a voice in her heart say, "It is all that is made." She wondered how such a small, seemingly insignificant thing could last, and the answer she received was, "It lasts and will last forever because God loves it, and in the same way everything exists through the love of God."

She realized three truths with this simple vision: first, God made the small, seemingly insignificant things; second, He loved them; and third, He cared for and watched over them. "Truly He is the maker, the lover and the care-er," she said and concluded the story with her personal surrender: "I can never have love, rest or true bliss until I am so bound to Him that there may be no created thing between my God and me."[3]

Julian knew that her act of brokenness, or surrender, could be accomplished only through the mercy and grace of God. Brokenness can be faked with appearances of humility and self-induced suffering. She didn't want that. She wanted to be real.

You and I, like Julian of Norwich, were created to surrender ourselves to God. We lovingly tell Him, "I surrender my life to You," and He enters that sweet surrender with His unmerited favor, and like a lifeguard assisting a struggling swimmer to shore, He carries us through to the full reality of our purpose on earth, even if the whole world has turned against us.

In 2012, at the President's Prayer Breakfast in Washington, DC, I met John Ramsey, a soft-spoken, unassuming man in his sixties, the father of a murdered six-year-old beauty queen, JonBenét Ramsey. The story of her murder in 1996 was, and still is, a media sensation. John and his wife, Patsy, were accused of murdering their little girl, and their life became an unthinkable nightmare. They lost everything they owned, and Patsy died of cancer before they were officially exonerated. I had the privilege of being the co-writer of his story for the book *The Other Side of Suffering*. I want to share with you a short piece from the book so you can hear what this gentle-hearted, kind man has to say of brokenness.

> In the nightmare of the loss of our little girl and Patsy's cancer I prayed for strength, for courage; I prayed God would spare the life of my wife. I can see now that what I've really been after is the Presence of God. Seeking His Presence is not about trying to get Him to do something. . . . I believe in every one of us there is a hunger for God. We may try to fill that hunger in many ways, but the only way it can be filled is by God Himself. Through Him, then, we go on to live our lives empowered by His Spirit. Through Him we reach our divine destiny. I have agonized over who killed JonBenét for fourteen years. I pray this monster will be found and brought to justice, but I am not twisted up in grief over the fact he's still out there. If the Boulder police toss up their hands and do nothing more to solve the murder, if the investigators throw the case into the cold files to go down as one of America's Most Notorious Unsolved Crimes, God is still on the throne.[4]

Possessed

The soul is happiest when possessed by God. That may seem like a simplistic statement, and so it is. The little seed, or nut, or whatever it was that Julian of Norwich saw in the palm of her hand is like you and me. We are small things, but in His hand we are infinite. We are eternally boundless in His love and care.

David said in Psalm 139:14, "I am marvelously made!" (Message), talking about the genius of God to create something as incredible as a human being. The New King James Version reads, "I am fearfully and wonderfully made." David wasn't flattering himself regarding his own physicality. "God so loved the world" (John 3:16) tells us God created all of us for Himself. He created us wonderfully for Himself. He didn't just throw together the creation of universes, galaxies, and humanity without knowing and planning what was best for us. He had a plan for that small thing in the palm of Julian's hand.

The truth is we're not really all that unique in our *human* condition. We're basically like every other human. What's the difference between the one in the world who achieves their goals and the one who doesn't? Nothing. It's *in God* we become truly unique. Possessed by Him, we're chosen, surrendered, unique treasures.

A Response to Being God's Beloved

As God's beloved, you possess His blessing. It's time to be grateful and celebrate. You can't celebrate when you're complaining. Look for small things to celebrate. The way your fingers move across the page of this book, the feel of sunlight on your neck, the sound of your breath. Pay attention to the small things and be grateful for them (Zech. 4:10).

In the practical world, we send a card or flowers to say thanks. What do we give the Lord? Nothing opens the gates of lasting happiness like gratitude. When you purpose in your heart to be grateful, you'll continually find more things to be grateful for. You'll no longer need answered prayer to be grateful for something to work out well (though we rejoice and celebrate these blessings!). Your personhood now and forever is His, and you can exclaim with a great sigh of grateful delight, "It is well with my soul." Studies conducted regarding the effects of gratitude on the overall well-being of a person are unanimously positive. They prove one thing: God created us to be grateful. A thankful heart is free to love life and be truly happy.

Gratitude has been shown to reduce health complaints too numerous to name, but I've had clients tell me their ulcers vanished, their headaches went away, their skin cleared up, and their bruxism (teeth grinding) ended. Gratitude must start and end your day.

Deep inside your grateful heart is the treasure you seek.

"For you are a holy people to the LORD your God, and the LORD has chosen you to be a people for Himself, a special treasure above all the peoples who are on the face of the earth" (Deut. 14:2). "But we have this treasure in earthen vessels that the excellence of the power may be of God and not of us" (2 Cor. 4:7).

The Loveaholic

Oh never leave me
My darling,
I can't live without you . . .

Do you recognize the familiar message in my little song lyric?
"You (human person) are my total all," "You (human unpredictable person) give me breath and life," and "Without you (human
fallible person) I simply can't go on." We hear this message every
day in music, the media, books, movies, culture, and the very air
we breathe.

I'm a fan of opera. I sob my heart out when Tosca, crying hys-
terically, realizes her lover, Mario, has been shot dead and then
leaps off the wall of the tower of Castel San Angelo to her own
death. And no matter how many times I see *Madame Butterfly*,
I fall apart when Cio-Cio San plunges the dagger into her heart.
These people die for human love. You'll see more people die for
love on the opera stage than anywhere else, except perhaps in a

Shakespearean play. What could be more sad than poor Romeo and Juliet lying dead in their youth, the whole world lamenting? Human love is passionately sad and tragic, and opera plays on our emotions to demonstrate that truth with artistic magnification. Human love is frail, fickle, and (gasp) deadly.

I saw the opera *La Bohème* for the first time as a young girl at the Paris opera house. I was by myself and had a box seat. I was so thrilled and excited to see Puccini's *La Bohème* in Paris that I arrived an hour early. I wore a really cute dress and sat enthralled from the first notes of the overture to the final act. But at the very end of the opera, that last moment when Rodolfo lets loose with a final cry of anguish, "Mimi!" for his dead loved one, I was so caught up with emotion that I nearly flew out of the box. I was absolutely overcome! Tears streamed down my face onto my really cute dress. I had only one tissue in my purse, and I was simply a wreck. When I leapt to my feet to applaud and shout bravos with the ecstatic French audience, I was dizzy. My knees trembled beneath me, and I could hardly breathe.

Poor Rodolfo. Poor Mimi. Human love. It'll kill you.

I'm talking about *human* love. Romantic love is in our DNA. We love it and long for it. God programmed us for romantic love, but He also programmed us for a love that goes deeper than romance. It's possible to live a beautifully rich and happy life without romantic love, but it's not possible to live a beautifully rich and happy life without the love of God. Romantic love is largely dependent on emotions, and we can live on the energy of our emotions for only so long. Human emotions aren't dependable. Art and life teach us that.

When Christ loves in us and through us, we're lifted to an entirely different plateau of human life. This is called *agape* love, and it can be attained and known only through Him. It's selfless, sacrificial, unconditional love that we're free to accept or reject. Someone who has this love voluntarily suffers inconvenience, discomfort, and even death for the benefit of another without expecting anything in return. *Agape* love isn't based on emotions, and it motivates us for action. The New Testament contains over two hundred references to this kind of love. "Therefore be imitators of God as dear children. And walk in love [*agape*], as Christ also has loved [*agaped*] us" (Eph. 5:1–2).

Do all lovers love one another with *agape* love? Of course not. If all happiness in the world depended on our loving God the way He loves us, it would be a miserable world because the world doesn't love God the way He asks us to. We experience love and happiness in the world because God loves the world.

The Loveless Place

Human love exists because God's love permeates the atoms and protons and nuclei of the world. Our life on earth with all that the earth offers is ours because God loves His world and He loves humanity. The sun rises on the evil and on the good, and rain falls on the just and the unjust (Matt. 5:45), so monk and felon alike enjoy the warmth of warm hugs and a sunny day.

The horror of hell as described in the Bible is that it's a place without so much as a hint of love. If a human soul rejects God and His love, naturally that soul will be drawn to, and become attached to, that which is godless. That's why the Bible tells us, "Choose for yourselves this day whom you will serve" (Josh. 24:15). Being without God doesn't mean you'll never enjoy goodness or happiness. These are possible without Him, of course, but they are contingent upon human ability, circumstances, environment, social situation, and luck, and they're not permanent. This book is about lasting happiness.

It stands to reason that those who choose shallow lives without God on earth will be drawn to an eternal spirit soul that matches theirs. That spirit soul is the ruler of hell, the devil, and he's prepared to lure and devour any human he can, and he does this first of all through the mind. "As he thinks in his heart, so he is" (Prov. 23:7). The devil wants your mind corrupted for hell.

The eternal soul who remains separated from God at death will, of course, remain separated from God after passing from this life. It's tragic because, once landing in hell, that soul will discover that whatever good they knew of life on earth was due to the love of God, whom they rejected. He can't be found in hell. Not even a glimpse of Him. God is love, and in hell there's no love. If your pursuit is to be in love, it's not love you seek; it's the Author of love.

Love versus Need

Lila talks about her marriage to her surgeon husband. "I feel like our marriage is all about him, not *us*. I worked two jobs for six years to put him through medical school. I literally wore myself ragged taking care of him. I'm still wearing myself out for him. Still taking care of him. My mother always told me if you make someone need you, they'll never leave you. I took her advice."

God intended for us to be whole and healthy human beings in ourselves, able to give the sweetest and best of ourselves to others. If you fill your inner self with a person, before you realize it, dependence sneaks up on you in the guise of love and, as in Lila's case, traps you in an all-about-the-other-person situation. Erich Fromm, in his classic book *The Art of Loving*, says, "We need to understand that we can only achieve love when we can stand alone as singly whole and secure persons. . . . Mature love is union under the condition of preserving one's integrity, one's individuality."[1] We're in trouble when we're incapable of standing alone in our integrity to freely love.

The first step in understanding how to love is to look at what you believe about love. What do you believe about love? Write it down in your happiness journal. Write what you don't believe about love. We're going to talk more about your ideas of love, but let's look first at the power of beliefs.

Some people believe that wearing garlic around their necks wards off colds and flu. Others believe drinking warm milk and garlic will ward off anything (and anyone, for that matter). We've heard we can get smarter by eating fish, stronger by eating spinach, thinner by eating grapefruit, and taller by taking our calcium.

The African Ashanti eat the hearts of their enemies because they believe doing so will give them courage. The Abipone of Paraguay believe eating jaguar flesh will give them speed. The Miri of Assam eat tigers to make themselves fierce.

What you *believe* dictates everything you do. Can you distinguish truth from error? From misbelief?

We've heard the heartsick, love-struck songs, and we're told that people who need people are lucky people. And then there's this touching thought: "I love you so much I could die." We're ready to buy into anything as long as it's in the name of something called love. We're too eager to accept false sentimentality and suffering and call it caring. It's good to be connected and a part of a caring world, but to be needy and desperate for love opens us up to abuse and unhappiness that could take years and even a lifetime to undo.

Love doesn't wound. Love doesn't drive you nuts. Love makes you more beautiful than you were before you found it. Love lifts you up to your best self. The essence of love is the ability to offer happiness to another. You can't offer happiness if you don't have happiness, just like you can't offer blessing if you aren't living in blessing.

With all respect to Lila's mother, her advice to her daughter to make her husband need her was not good advice. Need is not love, and God created us to be loved. After thirty years of being cared for by Lila, her spoiled and pampered husband left her for another woman.

Need can destroy a perfectly decent couple. They inflict pain on each other like unchaperoned children. Addicted to each other, they can't live without each other, yet they despise each other. If they continue with their addiction, they will destroy themselves and each other.

If you make somebody need you to the point where their well-being depends on you, that person will begin to dislike you and eventually hate you.

To believe people can fulfill our every need is about as realistic as believing that eating human hearts will give us courage and eating jaguar flesh will give us speed. We might consider such beliefs ignorant, but we treat our relationships with the same ignorance.

Writer James Thurber wrote that we are "brought up without being able to tell love from sex, Snow White, or Ever After. We think it [love] is a push button solution or instant cure for discontent and a sure road to happiness. By our sentimental ignorance we encourage marriage as a kind of tranquilizing drug."[2]

A loveaholic is

1. a dependent person
2. a person who makes another person dependent on them

The people who need drugs to feel good, caffeine to wake up, liquor to calm down, or a person to love them or need them in order to feel self-worth are unable to enter into the courts of lasting happiness. Happiness for them is fickle, easily dropped, and, like certain washable fabrics, quick to fade.

A major difference between someone who shows godly love and a loveaholic is that the loveaholic is not a giver. The loveaholic is a taker, even though they think they are a giver.

Love and Self-Worth

The ability to know our worth because we're loved by God has been maligned. We need to take a good, hard look at ourselves and the world that influences us. What does "I love you" really mean?

We treat love as though it existed somewhere apart from us, as though it falls on us from out of nowhere or we fall into it. I once heard the comedian Rita Rudner quip, "I've never fallen in love, but I've stepped in it a few times."

We know very little about love, and yet we're its slave. If we spend energy worrying about what we don't have and what's missing in our lives, we're ready for the loveaholic hotline. We'll look for someone else to boost our sense of worth, and we'll be ready to work hard to *earn* love and approval. Our misguided expectations are that we'll be rewarded for our hard work. It's time to discover how strong and beautiful we really are without anyone cheering us on and telling us what we want to hear.

Love between friends, spouses, siblings, co-workers, and fellow believers requires equal footing. When you lift someone up higher than you so that you feel subservient to them, examine your motive. When you choose someone beneath you to intimidate and control, examine your motive. Both of these instances demonstrate low self-esteem. Compare how you feel and act with someone who is on equal footing with you, with whom you feel right at home. What's the difference?

Your sense of worth and being a truly happy person depend on a foundational understanding of how you see yourself in God's eyes. This takes effort and awareness. Your authentic happy life does not rest in how others see and love you. Climb inside your heart and take a deep, penetrating look at what's inside. Inner work includes learning to sort through your needs to discard those that are destructive.

Change "I need you to love me the way I want to be loved!" to "I want to love you the way you want to be loved." (The word *need* is gone.)

Change "I need you to show me more attention" to "I want to show you loving attention because you deserve it, and I know you'll do the same for me." (Again, the word *need* is gone.)

Change your behavior and you change your life. Develop more meaningful ways of communicating by dropping accusations and demands. Put an end to the loveaholic reign of chaos and misery.

Lessons in Love

We learned our first lessons in love as children through our parents' approval or disapproval. We learned from their doting as well as their abuse. We learned from their indifference and abandonment as well as their caring and sharing. Our parents taught us about a world in which we must now decide how to live. They taught us what human love is and what it's not. Those early experiences, no matter how awful or good, influenced us, but the past is not our master.

Maybe your life now isn't as much fun as it was when you were a child, and you miss those sweet, happy years. Kenneth Grahame, the beloved author of many children's books, including *Wind in the Willows*, worked in a bank, and nostalgic for his happy childhood, he wrote down ideas for stories in his bank ledgers. Grahame published several wonderful books glorifying childhood. He was someone who saw childhood as a pleasure.

But perhaps your childhood was a nightmare you want to forget. If that is the case, the wounds of the past belong in the past. Often the most difficult task we face is ending our connection with the past and moving on to the joys and challenges of the present. It's common to treat the people in our lives today as if they were the ones who betrayed us or hurt us in the past. It's way too common not to trust today because of hurts we've gone through in the past.

Love is complicated, and we need to use all of our efforts and resources to create and maintain stable, constructive, beautiful relationships. Allowing your past a major role in any relationship is a mistake because it's the present, not your past, that holds the key to your future. Here are some pointers to help you overcome the past:

- Learn to see the beauty in all things.
- Recognize and question your learned patterns of behavior stemming from childhood.
- Choose to focus on your present life in terms of who you are today in Christ.

Write the following seven power statements in your happiness journal:

1. I'm complete in Christ.
2. I'm not my past. I'm fully alive in the present.
3. I'm worthwhile and lovable just as I am.
4. I stand alone before God as a whole person.
5. I have talents and abilities that God gives me because He expresses Himself through me.
6. I'm overflowing with good to give to the ones I love. My well never runs dry because the Lord is my continual supply.
7. I'm a person with self-esteem and integrity. I am me, just as God intended me to be.

These are powerful statements to remind yourself of every day. Don't remain stagnant or tangled in messed-up thinking. God's love is working and forming a new you; He's carving out an image of Himself in you. He says, "I accept you as you are. My wholeness creates wholeness in you."

True Love

In my book *Of Whom the World Was Not Worthy*, which takes place in former Yugoslavia, I wrote the true account of Jozeca and Jakob, a love story that exemplifies "love me for who I am and I will love you for who you are." This husband and wife went through World War II, prison, the birth of children, sickness, poverty, bitter cold, and hunger, and through it all, their love flourished. They lived in a world that was hostile and raging with war, death, and hunger, and their love had to stand alone, without outside encouragement. They had to be strong and sane. Integrity and equality were vital if they were to survive.

The loveaholic has little interest in the world outside their own small needs. The loveaholic shouts, "I can't get no satisfaction," and therein is the misconception that love originates and ends with frail and solipsistic human beings. It doesn't.

Here's a test for you to take to see how you measure up as a lover. Answer each of the following questions as honestly as you can. The "loved one" in the test can be a husband, wife, best friend, parent, son, or daughter—anyone you love.

1. Are you friends with the person you love most in your life?
2. Are you free of jealousy and possessiveness when your loved one's interests and activities aren't the same as yours?
3. Do you enjoy being alone and doing your own activity while the person you love engages in another activity?
4. Is your loved one's work nonthreatening to you?
5. Are you secure in yourself and your own value separate from anyone else?
6. Have you avoided giving up your own interests and becoming someone you're not in order to earn love?
7. Do you devote yourself to time alone for growth and spiritual renewal separate from your loved one?
8. Do you allow your loved one time away from you?
9. Do you want your loved one to be happy more than you want them to do what you want them to do?
10. Are you a better person—stronger, more compassionate, more giving—because of your relationship with your loved one?
11. Do you feel secure in your relationship even when you are not able to control it?

12. Are you uncritical toward your loved one if they don't do or think as you want?

Give yourself 2 points for every yes answer and score yourself as follows:

24–22 points: You're a lover who no doubt leads an exemplary life of nurturing and caring.

20–18 points: You could be in danger of hurting yourself and hurting someone else. Stop now and tell yourself, "I am a person of value. My loved one is a person of value. None of our thoughts or hearts are more precious than the other's. I choose to see us both as precious in the sight of God, and I refuse to put either of us down in any way, be it by action, word, or thought."

16 points or less: I know you're hurting. Go back to the seven power statements in this chapter and repeat them daily. Reread this chapter and tell yourself, "I am changing." Accept the fact that God wants your happiness and well-being because He loves you.

We need to love one another for who we are and stop demanding that others be what we neurotically think we need them to be. We need to stop our insistence that our loved ones fulfill a vacant hole in us. We need to see that what we believe to be passionate love may only be proof of our neediness and our loneliness.

According to 1 Corinthians 13:5, love doesn't seek its own. Love must seek God! If we don't know what love is, we're perpetually trying to find ways to gratify ourselves outside of God. We search for and grasp at people, things, and relationships, but we never find true love because love isn't self-centered. Love seeks not its own. A loveaholic is basically a self-centered, self-seeking person trying to find happiness through the commodity of love. But love is not a commodity for personal enrichment.

The word for loving-kindness in Hebrew is *hesed*, interpreted as "faithful love in action." It appears thirty times in the King James Old Testament, twenty-three times in the book of Psalms. It's a word with immense meaning because it surpasses general love or compassion. The word is relational, not general. It expresses a relationship with God. David understood that God's loving-kindness is better than life (Ps. 63:3) because he wasn't just an observer. He had a deep relationship with God.

The word *hesed* speaks of God's eternal covenant with Israel and with us who love Him. (A covenant is a promise, a legally binding divine document that can't be broken.) *Hesed* expresses God's loyalty and faithfulness to keep His promises. The Lord's loving-kindness indeed never ends, for His compassions never fail (Lam. 3:22). *Hesed* also means, because it's relational, that we, God's loved ones, are to be actively involved in His loving-kindness.

In the New Testament where the Greek word *eleos* is used for loving-kindness, it means "mercy." It's God's kindness and goodwill toward those who suffer. When we set ourselves free from a loveaholic mentality and lifestyle, we can shake ourselves off and start giving to others the benefits we experience as favored by God.

We float sweetly in the cool, clear waters of forgiveness, and God's *eleos*, His divine mercy, removes our guilt and shame. This is why Jesus proclaimed in the Sermon on the Mount, "Blessed are the merciful, for they shall obtain [divine] mercy" (Matt. 5:7). He wants us to show the same mercy toward everyone as He shows toward us. Reach outside yourself and your own human ability to show compassion and concern for someone in need. The apostle Paul never stopped interceding for others even when he was being persecuted. "It is more blessed to give than to receive," he said (Acts 20:35). That's the real you—a lover and a giver.

Before I leave this idea of *hesed*, let me suggest it as a fabulous way to start your day. The idea of mercy often occurs with morning in Scripture. Take a look for yourself. Check out these passages: Psalm 59:16; 90:14; 92:2; 143:8; Hosea 6:4; Lamentations 3:22–23. Praise God for His love to you, His beloved, each morning.

As you gain true love, you'll see your actions becoming more loving and outgoing, never vindictive or spiteful. Accept your new vulnerability. Plan to do and say loving things by writing them down.

1. At the top of a page in your happiness journal write, "The loving things I will say to my loved one(s) today." List as many as you can but no less than three.
2. Write in your happiness journal those behaviors that are decidedly childish as well as those that are of an overbearing parent. In writing them down, choose to end those behaviors.
3. Write down ten ways you're going to be a giver.
4. Carve out time in your day to simply sit in the presence of God in Quiet Prayer.

You're a person born to love and be loved. It's how you were created by God. Love is in your DNA. Be at home with this fact. To violate love, distort it, tamper with its sanctity, abuse it, and manufacture something else in its name will always bring discord, disharmony, and ultimately misery. It takes effort to truly understand in the depths of our souls who we are and why we're here, and to know lasting happiness in a world that doesn't value the love of God. When you begin to weed out the negative hurts and lies and tear down the loveaholic walls of neediness, the true light of pure love will always shine through into your life. See yourself today through God's eyes as his child fully loved, born to give and share that love.

Heart and Soul Happiness

If you want to see a perfect example of miserable, unhappy people, look at the Pharisees in the Bible. What a grim lot they were. A grumbling, negative, faithless group of unhappy men. Their poor wives.

This chapter looks at where happiness thrives in us. We've seen that the root of our lasting happiness is Christ's life in us by His Spirit, and I've introduced Quiet Prayer as a route to reach the depths of intimacy with Him. Now I want to point out the amazing totality of who you are and how lasting happiness can sprout and prosper in both your heart and soul.

The Place of Faith

Nothing beautiful happens to us spiritually without faith. Everything starts with faith. With faith all things are possible. Without faith nothing is possible. Jesus said more than once, "Your faith has made you whole." We're made whole in every way, not only physically when our bodies are healthy but also in our souls. We're whole in our thinking, our emotions, our inclinations, our decisions, our attitudes.

I told you at the beginning of this book that happiness is a skill we teach ourselves. Faith is the function that initiates new life and the journey to the unfathomable riches of happiness that lasts. Without faith, let me say right off, none of this is possible.

Where does faith reside in you? The answer is everywhere, but it starts in the soul. First, you absorb the initial gleanings of faith by means of your mind. Faith channels through your mind until it reaches the heart, where you feel things. Now you have thinking, feeling faith. And from there it expands into the other faculties of your soul. Your soul is your mind, your emotions, and your will. It includes your personality, your desires, your talent, your intellect, the full spectrum of your emotions, and your will. Like a sweet summer breeze swirling about, faith reaches into your heart and soul and takes flight. But that's not the end of it.

Your human heart, soul, and mind need to connect with the heart, soul, and mind of the Holy Spirit of God. Every believer is familiar with the story of Nicodemus (a Pharisee, by the way), who made a secret visit at night to ask the Lord serious questions about faith. Jesus told him that we're born once in human flesh and blood, but we need to be born *again* by the Holy Spirit of God. It's then, when our human spirit is made alive by His Holy Spirit, that we have the potential to become our true self because we have God *in us* connecting to every part of our being.

Let's look at faith's itinerary as it moves through these human frames. Faith comes to you first through your mind. You see or hear something that impresses you, and you accept whatever it is as true or real, and you believe that it is what it says it is or does. People either believed Jesus was who He said He was, or they didn't. They either believed what He preached, the miracles He performed, or they didn't. They had faith in Him, or they didn't. Faith happens first in the mind.

Some people can remain in their mind for a lifetime, never allowing their faith to seep into their heart. Their life of faith is strictly intellectual, mental. They can talk about God day and night, study the Scriptures in both Greek and Hebrew, but their faith stays fixed in their intellect, which is only one component of their soul. They become better critics than lovers.

This kind of assenting faith doesn't move mountains. An intellectual believer isn't usually motivated to pray for miracles or to walk in the supernatural realm. And happiness is something that comes and goes depending on circumstances. This is the person who says it's not possible to have lasting happiness because they have no reference in the laboratory of their mind as to what that means. They lack the faith to believe there's a life of happiness above the cares and trials of the world.

From the fertile ground of your mind, your faith moves into your heart. It lodges there and then leaps across the mountains and valleys of your reasoning and senses. It captures your human soul (your intellect, emotions, will, thoughts, ideas, talents, personality), and then beautifully and gloriously, if you surrender to Him completely, sweeps the totality of you up in the magnificent power of the Holy Spirit, and you're completely alive. When the totality of you is ignited by His power and presence, your human spirit is ignited by His Holy Spirit, and nothing is impossible to you.

When Jesus was on earth, He could tell instantly who had faith for miracles and who didn't even before anyone said a word to Him. When the woman healed of the issue of blood touched the fringe of His robe, for instance, He *felt* her faith (Matt. 9:20–22). He physically felt the faith of this woman. She didn't speak two words to Him; she didn't even look Him in the eye. She reached down and simply touched the bottom fringe of his robe, in Hebrew called the *tzitzit*. She didn't touch *Him*, and she didn't touch the *robe*; she touched the *tzitzit* of the robe. He bolted around in the crowd, exclaiming, "Who touched Me? Somebody touched Me—I perceived power going out from Me!"

Jesus *felt* the woman's faith. Faith in God that has dynamically moved into the heart of a human being cannot only be seen—it can be felt. The woman was healed immediately when Jesus said to her, "Be of good cheer, daughter; your faith has made you well" (v. 22).

Jesus also restored the sight of two blind men in Matthew 9:29, telling them, "According to your faith let it be to you." He sensed their faith in Him and knew their faith had already healed them before He proclaimed it to them.

Faith wants to pervade every area of your life. Paul prayed for the believers at Ephesus that they "know the love of Christ which passes knowledge [beyond what the human mind and intellect can figure out]" and that they be "filled with all the fullness of God" (Eph. 3:19). Whole means complete.

Does becoming alive in the Spirit assure us of happy lives on earth? The answer is yes and no. I've known many miserable Christians. Though they were born again, they became stagnant through lack of spiritual participation, action, and effort. They didn't read or study the powerful, positive promises and life-building words of the Bible; their prayer lives were empty; they rarely spent much time alone with God; and their minds were fixed on the cares of the world, not what God says about the cares of the world. They simply didn't allow themselves to know and love God.

I also know some of the happiest people on earth, dynamic, gloriously anointed, blessed believers who have grasped the principles of lasting happiness that I'm teaching you in this book. To be in the presence of these dear saints of God is a gift. My life is made richer for them, and so is the world.

Layers of the Heart

You have a beautiful heart. The Old Testament mentions the heart 860 times. It is the place in us where both evil and good reside. It is also where the Word of God meets us. "But the word is very near you, in your mouth and in your heart, that you may do it" (Deut. 30:14).

The word *heart* is translated as "the inner person" fifteen times in the New Testament. Think of your heart as housing certain aspects of your soul, such as your passions, desires, inclinations, and longings. "Pharaoh hardened his heart" (Exod. 8:15)—referring to his place of no compassion. "Let not your heart be troubled" (John 14:1)—referring to where emotional panic can arise. "I will praise You, O Lord my God, with all my heart" (Ps. 86:12)—referring to the whole of your passion.

The heart is like an onion; it has layers. Each layer contains and embodies certain qualities of ourselves that God uses to mold and fit us into Himself, into His personality. He shapes us to fit our spirits into His desires, passion, and purposes.

The Outward Layer of the Heart

This is the layer of our outer selves that we present to the world. We make this decision within us. We don't just accidentally look or appear a certain way. We choose how we present our physical selves to the world.

The first aspect of this outer layer is how much attention we give to how we carry ourselves and what choices we make in how we carry ourselves. I have a friend, Sharon Libby, with post-polio syndrome, and she is confined to a wheelchair. She's probably one of the most active, vibrant Christians I know. The outer layer of her heart is beautiful because she has made it so and she is at home with who she is physically. What we tell ourselves about our outer layer tells us much about what's underneath.

Viktor Frankl, whom I quoted in chapter 1, survived terrible torture in the Holocaust, and to his torturers he said, "The one thing you can't take away from me is the way I choose to respond to what you do to me."[1] The outer layer of his heart in the death camp did not shrivel or shatter under pain; he was not afraid of pain. He was outwardly tortured in the nightmare of the Auschwitz concentration camp, but his heart stayed intact.

Your body responds to what you tell yourself. It responds to the self-talk you engage in with physical weariness, aches and pains, sickness and brokenness, but also with vibrant health and vigor. You can choose to fold over and disintegrate, or you can rise up strong and determined. You wear the pain and drama of your life on your body. Your body pays the price for how much effort you invest in the beauty and strength of your soul.

The Second Layer of the Heart

This is the layer where you give your attention and enthusiasm to what you believe. This is your passion layer. Here is where you strip off that which drains your energies, that which drains you of life, that which drains you of your clear, holy vision in God. The mind-set is more intent on God and less on your outer image.

When you enter Quiet Prayer every day in the secret place and grow more intimate with God, you'll become more excited about Him and who He is inside you. It will become easier for you to recognize the things that rob you of joy. You'll become more able to identify the things that drain you of energy and the things that fill you with energy. It's here in this layer of the heart where you begin to really take care of your spiritual walk in Christ. Hold your Quiet Prayer time as sacred and learn the meaning of Galatians 5:1: "Stand fast therefore in the liberty by which Christ has made us free, and do not be entangled again with the yoke of bondage."

The Third Layer of the Heart

This layer is the protective layer. You've become more vulnerable in your faith. You realize your enthusiasm and openness, which are infectious, could bring you hurt. This layer of the heart is vulnerable to breaking and can show itself when you become defensive, telling yourself, "I'll never be hurt again," or "I don't trust anybody," or "It's always the good guys who get shafted." This is the layer that can block out the light. It's where you might fall back into the ruts of "I can't" and "poor me."

But this is also where you can rejoice in your safety. At this level, the verse, "You will keep him in perfect peace whose mind is stayed on You" (Isa. 26:3) comes alive. The apostle Paul said he learned to be at peace in all situations: "I have learned in whatever state I am, to be content" (Phil. 4:11). At this level, you can know a deeper contentment and peace in trusting who God is and who you are in Him because you're safe.

The Fourth Layer of the Heart

This is your truth layer. It's here where your knowledge and experience merge with your spirit and your life reflects not only your integrity but also your walk with God. This layer of your heart contains the years of what the world has taught you together with what God has taught you. Sometimes the world has been your major teacher, and God has ranked second in influence. You can change that right now if that's the case. If your truth layer is slim on the God side, you can increase your understanding. Proverbs 3:5 tells us we aren't to lean on our own understanding, which is futile; we'd be much happier if we trusted in the Lord with all our heart. If you acknowledge (recognize and honor) Him in all your ways, He (not the world around you) will direct your path.

This layer of your heart demonstrates what you've taught yourself to believe. Jesus told His disciples to grab hold of (possess) the words He spoke and *live* in them. See yourself climbing into the Word of God as though it were a tent, its walls snug around you. The Word of God is actually a "He" because Jesus is the Word (John 1:1). When you open your Bible and enter its words, you're absorbing the presence of Jesus Himself into your heart, mind, and spirit—your inner parts. Don't underestimate what's taking place in you when you read the Word.

In Psalm 51:6, David prayed, "Behold, You desire truth in the inward parts, and in the hidden part You will make me know wisdom." Jesus said we will know the truth and the truth will make us free (John 8:32). It's *knowing* that counts. Your heart needs to be filled with truth in order for you to be made a free person from the inside out and in every aspect of your life.

David prayed in Psalm 26:2, "Examine me, O LORD, and prove me; try my mind and my heart." When God looks at your heart, He sees the level of truth you live in. When you know the truth, you live in the truth. That's why David could proclaim in Psalm 27:1, "The LORD is the strength of my life; of whom shall I be afraid?" When the truth has lodged triumphantly in your heart, made its home there, you'll see that you live inside God's loving-kindness and you will be fearless.

The heart is the place of courage and also where fear does its havoc if you allow it to. Fear of tomorrow, fear of dying, fear of being alone, fear of hard work, fear of pain, fear of rejection—all of these ferment to condemn your beautiful heart. But there's a way out! God says if your heart condemns you, not to worry. He is much greater than your heart, and He knows all things (1 John 3:20). This is the demonstration of His wisdom, as he forges the path for mercy and righteousness to become sealed in your personality and character (Pss. 117:2; 119:160; Prov. 3:3).

The Fifth and Final Layer of the Heart

Here's where you were born to live. "And we have known and believed the love that God has for us. God is love, and he who abides in love abides in God, and God in him" (1 John 4:16).

Here's the fire, the flame, and the core of your being. It's where everything you are emanates from. It's the eternal seed and center of your being. As much of God as you have in this deep center core is as much as you'll know who you are. We can exist day in and day out without being present in our own lives. Don't let it happen to you. As you unwrap the layers of your heart, consider yourself the most blessed person on the planet. Be present in yourself. Whatever circumstances you're in right now, be present in them exactly as things are.

We've been taught to think that wisdom is something that's birthed and nurtured in the mind. We think of wisdom as a reasoning ability, but wisdom lives in the heart. When young Solomon became king after his father, David, he prayed for an understanding heart, and it pleased God greatly. Solomon didn't pray for a smart, clever brain. He prayed for an understanding heart, a listening heart (1 Kings 3:9).

The verse, "Delight yourself also in the LORD, and He shall give you the desires of your heart" (Ps. 37:4) is telling you to let go of every hassle of the heart and let wisdom emerge. Wisdom always delights in the Lord, for He is wisdom. Open the petals of your heart and delight yourself. The verse says *you* do it. You delight in the Lord. You. Purpose in your heart to enter the presence of the Lord and there, in His magnificence, to delight in Him.

Where your heart is, your treasure is (Matt. 6:21). Your treasure doesn't exist outside of you; it is *in* you. You carry your treasure around in you. You go to bed at night with it in you. You play tennis with your treasure in you. You shop, eat, dance, play, work, and pray with your treasure right there inside your heart.

How big is your treasure?

Choosing Happiness

You can see by what we've examined so far that happiness is something we choose. Something we purposely work at possessing. Your beautiful heart and soul are more than just a bunch of feelings at the whim of events, circumstances, and people. To know lasting happiness requires all of your attention—body, soul, and spirit.

Faith doesn't exist out there on a limb waiting for you to come pluck some up when things go wrong; faith lives in you and it needs daily nourishing. Your heart and soul crave it. Faith inspires wisdom, wisdom inspires gratitude, gratitude inspires delight, and delight inspires the truly happy soul.

Your Happy Brain

When looking back on your life, or even the events of the past week, do you remember the happy or unhappy moments most? Neuroscience research tells us that we are hardwired to register and remember negative events more quickly and deeply than positive ones, which creates an unhappy brain.

A happy brain is shaped differently than an unhappy one, but neuroscience and the Bible tell us that through training exercises, an unhappy brain can be molded to actually look like a happy one. Neuropsychologists explain the concept as neuroplasticity, specifically how the brain's physical shape can be changed. The shape of the brain can be changed under the influence of external events. Members of the grin-and-bear-it club can remain as they are hardwired, or they can choose to change.

How Your Brain Works

In the beginning, God designed the human brain for beauty, joy, love, and trust, but when Adam fell and was removed from the

Garden of Eden, his brain mechanism had to adjust to a different environment, an environment of danger and pain. Out in the cold, cruel world and no longer blissfully unaware of danger or evil, Adam had to contend with those things.

His world was no longer perfect. His brain, therefore, had to adjust to anticipate and overcome dangers. Adam's brain became a tool to protect him from pain and to figure out ways to solve problems. The brain became negatively biased. As a result, dangers, pains, and problems are the events that capture our brain's attention to this day. The human nervous system, Rick Hanson writes, "scans for, reacts to, stores, and recalls negative information about oneself and one's world. The brain is like Velcro for negative experiences and Teflon for positive ones; the natural result is a growing—and unfair—residue of emotional pain, pessimism, and numbing inhibition in implicit memory."[1]

The brain makes distinctions between two types of memory: implicit and explicit. Explicit memory empowers us to do things like remember the names of our friends or where we parked the car. On the other hand, implicit, or emotional, memories are formed unconsciously. These memories are viscerally rather than logically initiated.

The amygdala of the brain, which is an almond-shaped set of neurons deep in the brain's temporal lobe, acts as the switchboard in implicit memory as it responds to outside stimuli. It's neurologically primed to label experiences as frightening and threatening. Once the amygdala flags an episode as negative, it immediately stores the event and compares it to the record of old, painful experiences. If a match is found, a series of chemical reactions signals alarm. These events occur to protect us from harm, but as a result, the bad things that happen are registered and responded to almost instantaneously, whereas the happy events take five to twenty seconds just to begin to register. The daily stress you live with is perceived by your brain as a literal battle for survival. The swirl of chemical reactions due to stress dictates the brain's helpless, persistent focus on negativity.

We need to deliberately rewire our brain. Leading a genuinely happy life doesn't happen without our deliberate effort or retraining our brain. For most people, agitation, anger, and fear are easier to access and sustain than peace, happiness, and fulfillment. That is why this book is aimed at teaching you *new* skills.

Deliberate effort is a function of the higher regions of the brain. In one fascinating study, researchers took brain scans of people who regularly engaged in some form of meditation and meditative prayer and those with no meditation experience. After an eight-week meditation program, researchers found that not only did the higher brain regions thicken but the amygdala also became less dense with the praying people. They were happier. Now wellness health centers are offering different forms of meditation to patients to protect them against stress-related disorders and depression.

It's that easy? We should pray more?

Yes.

The Beautiful Effects of Quiet Prayer

Neuroscientists have discovered that human beings who practice prayer and meditation are happier people than those who do not. Prayer, of all things! Not a better environment, not health, not DNA, not social status, not money, not success, not wealth but prayerful meditation makes people happier.

Hinduism, Buddhism, and movements such as Transcendental Meditation use their form of meditation to *empty* the mind. For Christians, however, meditation is filling the heart and mind with the presence of God and His Word. David prayed, "The meditation of my heart shall give understanding" (Ps. 49:3). Quiet Prayer is a form of Christian contemplative meditation. It's the process of entering the presence of God, as David explains in Psalm 145:5: "I will meditate on the glorious splendor of Your majesty, and on Your wondrous works."

When you practice Quiet Prayer as a part of your daily life, you connect with God with the very depths of your heart. Think of closing the door of your busy, active mind and choosing another faculty to communicate with God by letting your heart connect with Him. The God of the Bible is a personal God who desires a personal, intimate relationship with us. Quiet Prayer is in direct response to the love of God, as in 1 John 4:19: "We love Him because He first loved us." We're so accustomed to chatter and clamor, to endless talking, that to sit still and simply focus on God with a wordless heart is a new experience. In most of us, this depth of our heart has been untapped. Only the outer layers have been broken through.

The Hebrew words for meditation in the Old Testament are *hagah*, which means "to sigh or murmur" but also "to meditate," and *sihah*, which means "to muse or rehearse in one's mind." When the Hebrew Bible was translated into Greek, *hagah* became the Greek *melete*, which expressed meditation's effects on the depth of the human heart.

Meditate and *meditation* appear in the Bible about twenty times, fifteen times in the book of Psalms. One of my favorite verses throughout my life has been Joshua 1:8, which has new meaning for me now since I'm learning the power of Quiet Prayer.

> This Book of the Law shall not depart from your mouth, but you shall meditate in it day and night, that you may observe to do according to all that is written in it. For then you will make your way prosperous, and then you will have good success.

Quiet Prayer doesn't take the place of studying the Word of God with pen and notebook, reading, notating, memorizing, and taking part in Bible studies and prayer gatherings. It's in addition to these. As your mind is stilled, a sweet transformation and inner growth take place that you carry with you in your daily life and callings.

Another category of quieting the clattering, chattering mind is the practice of holy awareness, as I introduced in chapter 4. I call it holy because there's something sacred about the act of being fully alive and fully present. Holy awareness is a how-to-be-happy-in-an-unhappy-world life skill, and it means to fully experience the sensory world—seeing, hearing, tasting, smelling, feeling—and to be aware of the moment and the holiness of it.

Holy awareness and meditation are alike in many ways, and both celebrate the presence of God. Purposefully paying attention deeply, and without judgment, to whatever arises in the present moment, either inside or outside of us, takes effort.

Creating New Patterns

Now that you recognize the negative patterns you've formed in your brain in response to pain (physical or emotional), you can learn new patterns of response. Most of our lives are spent fighting pain, reacting in flight or fight at the appearance of pain. Anger, indignation, fear, self-blame, and depression usually overtake us. For this reason, we need to combat the misbeliefs associated with pain and practice kindness and compassion first toward ourselves. You can't offer love and respect to someone else unless you possess love and respect for yourself. Learn to practice awareness in such a way that you can create moments of contentment and peace wherever you are. When you nourish yourself, you can nourish another.

Here's a short self-compassion practice for you. When dealing with pain (physical or emotional), take yourself to a quiet place, close your eyes, and allow your body to become still. Allow your body to release all tension. Breathe deeply. Remain this way for a few minutes, simply breathing.

Imagine the Lord Jesus entering the room or wherever you are.

Imagine Him smiling at you and opening His arms to you.

Imagine Him placing His arms around you and holding you close.

Stay there in His arms while breathing deeply and evenly.

Imagine Him speaking to you:

> I love you with an everlasting love.
>   I hold you in My arms with loving-kindness;
> today feel My perfect heart of mercy embrace your dear
>   heart.
>   I embrace and love every part of you.
> I am drawing you closer to Me because I love you.
>   I am with you always.
> I am your healer, your deliverer.
>   I give you all of Me. My dearest, My own.[2]

As we learn to be aware of our negative reactions to pain, we have a choice to take a different path, the path of compassion and kindness. We build new neural pathways in our brains.

Build new brain habits of compassion and kindness toward yourself first and then toward others. When we reach down to the roots of our souls where we all cry together, we discover real kindness. If we can grow to a point in this world where we inhabit truth wholly, we'll come to know a deeper love and kindness for everyone on the road with us.

These new reactions hold you up in the face of difficulty and stress. You develop habits of mind and heart that can't be disturbed, even under great strain. "I shall not be moved" becomes your reality because you have developed courage through pain and can rise up strong with the firm, deep knowledge of your safety and surety in Christ. "I can do all things through Christ who strengthens me" (Phil. 4:13) is more than an encouraging statement. It's the bone and marrow of your life.

Your faith is not based on willpower; you're not white-knuckling it through life. Rather, you face what's present in the moment, accepting the situation even if it means opening yourself to a painful or unpleasant experience, and see it exactly as it is. At this point of engagement, you look for the misbeliefs in your inner dialogue, or self-talk, that may be associated with the moment. "This is bad." "I hate this." "Why did this happen to me?" "How could God let this happen?"

Hear what you tell yourself. Then counter your misbeliefs with the truth:

God turns bad to good, evil to righteousness, mourning to dancing.

This may not be pleasant, but I can accept it.

I'm surrounded with God's love at all times and through all things.

God knows me better than I know myself. He holds me in His arms.

As you sit with increasingly difficult experiences, you'll discover the ability to overcome and rise up stronger than ever through the indwelling power of the Holy Spirit within you. Does this take faith? Yes.

Pastor Steven Furtick of Elevation Church in Charlotte, North Carolina, says too many of us suffer from what he calls posttraumatic faith disorder. He says, "A lot of Christians I know stagger through life in a daze. Suffering from posttraumatic faith disorder, they hunker down in the basement, open a can of Beanie Weenies, and wait for the end of the world."[3]

Faith makes you unshakable. Faith shows you the impermanence of this world and the eternity of God. Picture yourself as a mountain, unshakable through battering storms, deluges, the plundering of man, changes of nature. Unshakable. That's you.

And that's happiness.

When I was going through a particular dark hour of the soul, a girlfriend took me by the shoulders and drilled into me, "Marie, you are going to do three things to feel better! Here they are. One, you are going to get dressed every day. That means you are going to put on your makeup and look good. Two, you are going to answer your email and phone calls. Three, you are going to show up somewhere!"

That was so practical it hurt. But I begrudgingly tried to do as she suggested. I got up and got dressed every day. I put on my makeup. I answered email and phone calls. But the third thing—show up—well, not so much.

Studies have shown that 80 percent of personal happiness and success starts with showing up. Workers rise to the top of their companies by showing up and faithfully doing their jobs. Preachers, priests, and pastors show up to church; athletes show up for practice; actors show up for rehearsals and drama classes. Happily, my mother showed up for her wedding when she married my dad. My doctor showed up when I broke my neck in a bike accident. Friends have shown up when I've needed them.

I thought about it and miserably started showing up. I showed up at my computer to write, I showed up at the gym to work out, I showed up at church and at school. I showed up. No expectations of myself. No to-do lists of how to show up. I just showed up.

When you don't feel like showing up, do as I did and grab the hand of God and head out the door. How many times do we doubt ourselves and feel we can't do the task at hand? Grab the hand of God and show up.

I felt good about myself for doing what I didn't want to do. Soon the darkness began to lift, and I was brought back to the reality of a life without fear. And I was grateful. The clouds parted and happiness was in sight.

Growth is a beautiful thing. Treasure your growth. Honor your growth. Inside a newborn baby is unlimited potential. Walking is inside that baby. Running is inside him. Speech is inside him. Words, laughter, thought, caring, loving—all inside.

In the same way, that person you pray to be already exists inside you. If you listen really hard, you'll hear your own voice calling you forward into your wonderful future. The Bible says as a man thinks, so he is (Prov. 23:7), which means if you can think a thing, the pathway to reach it is already in motion. The reality of achieving what you see ahead is in you!

This is exactly how we spiritually train our minds and our hearts. We *train* ourselves to be happy and live happy lives. We *live* our training. Our human brains are wired to lean toward negativity, but God has created human brains to be rewired. Think of yourself as in the process of rewiring your brain. You're developing permanent changes by taking radical action. You are choosing to see that with God you're alive, mindful, and no longer a victim of circumstances, events, situations, or relationships. You're in serious happiness training. You can change. You can turn from old habits and form new ones. Neuroscience studies show us that brain training can turn unhappy minds into happy ones.

Real Happiness

Don't compromise your happiness. If you compromise and accept less than God has for you, you'll know it. You'll feel it. You'll know it when you've settled for less. Don't sacrifice the permanent on the altar of the temporary. I realize how easy it is to compromise, to accept the cheap, fleeting perks the world offers. But real happiness isn't some fly-by-night thing.

Happiness involves being strong, tough, resilient. The world isn't getting any nicer or any happier. We hear bad news from every corner of civilization, so we must be resilient. We must be able to stand up strong when the winds of chaos strike. We can't do that unless we know how to stay happy.

I don't mean shallow happiness that comes and goes. I'm talking about developing and holding on to a happy heart that experiences life in this troubled world with wisdom, character, courage, and understanding through God.

"A merry heart does good, like medicine," it says in Proverbs 17:22. A happy heart is your cupful of vitamins and your mood elevator. A happy heart lives in your brave and courageous self. No amount of bad news from the world can tear down your happy heart. Jesus isn't pulling out His hair and biting His fingernails up in heaven over the condition of our world. On the contrary, He's busy empowering His children to overcome darkness and light up the world!

Miserable people cast no light. Grumpy, complaining people cast no light. Moody, selfish people cast no light. Angry people cast no light. Anxious, fearful people cast no light. You are the light of the world, remember.

Let me tell you about a client of mine. He was a guy who believed the unhappy world was to blame for his problems in life. He assiduously followed the news and received regular disaster messages through the internet and social media. He kept tabs on terrorism attacks, flu epidemics, airplane crashes, prayer banished in the schools, and criminal activity both locally and nationally. He felt he was doing humankind a service by keeping up with the times and got frustrated when his wife and children placed demands on him. He couldn't understand why they weren't more supportive of what he considered a calling to keep people informed. He saw himself as a giving, unselfish, faithful Christian, but in reality he was functioning with an unbridled case of inferiority. Turning his attention from himself and his needs gave him a feeling of relief, and the emotional high he received from being outraged at world events fed a false sense of self-importance.

He didn't talk about God's goodness or mercy. He didn't talk about God's power or His purposes in these times. Instead, he concentrated on wrath, on judgment, on the perilous end times. He thrived on bad news, though God is on the throne and the word *gospel* means good news. His devil was bigger than his God.

Our Christian leaders and pastors continually cry out for God's people to pray. God is telling us, "If My people who are called by My name will humble themselves and pray," not "If My people will lose sleep over the world situation and worry themselves to pieces." Here's the entire verse: "If My people who are called by My name will humble themselves, and pray and seek My face, and turn from their wicked ways, then I will hear from heaven, and will forgive their sin and heal their land" (2 Chron. 7:14).

Try a media fast. If you catch yourself getting sidetracked and focusing your attention on the evils in the world, turn off the TV and the radio, set aside the newspapers, and go on a media fast. See if you can fast from all world news for one solid week. During that week, devote the time you ordinarily spend online, watching and reading news reports, and talking about the events of the day, to God and His Word. Ask Him for a revelation of His power and purpose in these times. Look for supernatural assurance from Him and find rest in the faith that He's in control. Pray 2 Chronicles 7:14 every day for your country.

The threat of terrorism, nuclear war, germ warfare, disease, and economic collapse loom before us. Add these global calamities to personal problems and disasters in the family, community, and church, and we're overloaded with enough worries and burdens to last until the next millennium. You and I have been called to live in "such a time as this" (Esther 4:14), and not as wimps sniveling in corners and begging for protection from above. "My help comes from the LORD who made heaven and earth" (Ps. 121:2), and He lives in you! The salient, urgent message of how to be happy in an unhappy world is that you have what you need within you! Christ in you, the hope of glory!

Yes, God will send His angels to watch over you and guide you. Yes, He will protect you by His Holy Spirit. Yes, He will provide for you and keep you safe. Yes, He is your deliverer and fortress, your strong tower. If God is for you, who can be against you? The Lord is your shepherd, and therefore you shall not want for anything! (Ps. 23:1). "My help comes from the LORD who made heaven and earth," and that help is inside you. God is calling His people to rise up strong in these times. I'm praying for you as you read this book that God is equipping you to rise up supernaturally strong and find lasting happiness no matter what happens.

Releasing Stored Memories

Fixating on the nightmares of the world surrounding you does more to you than just fill your mind with negativity. It affects you physically as well. Your body stores emotional memories. Science, medicine, and psychology show that the human body traps such emotions as stress, unforgiveness, fear, and anger. We know that certain physical maladies are directly related to emotional problems and turmoil.

The brain contains about sixty neuropeptides, which are the means by which all cells in the body communicate with one another. This includes brain-to-body messages. Individual cells, including brain cells, immune cells, and other body cells, have receptor sites that receive neuropeptides. The kinds of neuropeptides available to cells are constantly changing depending on your emotions, both positive and negative.

Cellular memory is the collective energy generated by individual cell memories. I'm not talking about when an amputated leg gives a person what's called ghost pain, nor am I talking about subconscious memories that respond to electric impulse. I'm talking about painful, toxic emotions that are stored in the body on a cellular level.

If you magnify your cells down to their atoms, you'd see that you are made up of subtle bundles of "info-energy." This info-energy comprises physical, mental, and emotional data that comes from all of your life experiences. Nothing you experience escapes being imprinted into your cells in the form of a cell memory.

You need to empty your mind and your body of the effects that painful experiences have had on you. For example, when you think back on a painful experience, you may call up certain painful emotions. Take a deep breath and give your body a soothing message of release from the physical response to that day in your life. You might say something like, "I free my body now of holding on to the pain of that day in the name of Jesus." Continue to speak freedom and healing to your body.

You may still be carrying the emotional pain of past painful experiences somewhere in your body, and you need to free yourself. Lack of forgiveness also stores itself somewhere in your body. If you carry bitterness or unforgiveness around in your heart, you've poisoned not only your heart and soul but also your body.

If you've been abused or injured, take time now to pray over those areas of your body. Release God's blessing on your body. Free your body from the memories and emotional pain it's storing. Thank your body for being good to you, for keeping you alive, for serving you.

I'm not saying that all physical toxicity is due to toxic experiences and emotions, but you can be certain your body is carrying around baggage and begging you for relief. That relief can come only from the Lord because the relief is spiritual.

Our glands, organs, tissues, and cells are storage places for emotional memory, as demonstrated through the scientific research of neuropharmacologist Dr. Candace Pert, who worked at the NIH and Georgetown University Medical Center. In her research, she wrote that our bodies are our subconscious minds and can be changed by the emotions we experience. "In being expressed, emotions can be released, even old emotions stored in body memory."[4] The body-mind is far more attentive than we realize. It doesn't miss a thing. The secret place of Quiet Prayer is a wonderful place to focus on letting go and releasing the trapped, stored, painful emotional memories in your body.

The man I spoke of earlier who was fixated on bad news lived with fierce emotional pain, not realizing what his inordinate interest in world disasters was doing to his body as well as his mind. Not only was he temperamental and moody, but his body also showed signs of the emotional baggage it carried. At thirty-eight years old, he suffered from arthritis, allergies, and insomnia. It was urgent he go on a media fast.

I'm happy to say he did! His wife says the media fast changed their life. God spoke to his heart during his media fast, and the

Holy Spirit entered his body, soul, and spirit in an awakening he'd never experienced. With Quiet Prayer twice a day, he was able to quiet his mind and hear from God. He's still interested in world events, but he says he only wants to see things through the eyes of God. He's working at releasing the negative memories stored in his body, and the last time I spoke with him, he no longer needed medication to put him to sleep at night.

Aging, Happiness, and Your Beautiful Brain

How many old people do you know who are vibrant with happiness? My great-aunt Anna was one hundred years old and still as sweet as cake, giggly and full of humor to the very last days of her life. She was a well-loved centenarian, and my children, who were in elementary school, loved visiting her. She was fun! Not only was she fun, but she also listened. I could curl up beside her and talk for hours.

My mother was in her nineties when she died. She became a writer of romance fiction, and up to the very end, she was full of ideas for new books to write. All her life she had physical problems, but nothing ever seemed to stop her. She worked hard, laughed hard, and created a happy, blessed atmosphere around her. She was dearly loved by everyone who knew her. Like my great-aunt Anna, she was fun!

But then there are the curmudgeons, the nasty, mean-spirited oldsters who find fault with everything, complain constantly, and give nothing back to the world. It's a tragedy really, because the brain can forge new pathways to happiness, and everyone at any age can live productive, fulfilling lives and give something back to the world. It's never too late to start giving back.

Frank Lloyd Wright was ninety years old when he designed the Guggenheim Museum. It was a milestone of architecture when it opened in New York City. No museum in the world was like it.

Here's another example. A woman named Mary Fasano went back to school at the age of seventy-one to earn her high school diploma and hit the news media eighteen years later when, at eighty-nine years old, she graduated with her undergraduate degree from Harvard University. She became the oldest person to earn a degree from Harvard.

In the college writing course I taught at Mira Costa College, I had a ninety-year-old retired psychiatrist take the class one semester. My young students loved her.

David Ben-Gurion, the first prime minister of Israel, taught himself ancient Greek in old age to master the classics in the original.

Benjamin Franklin invented bifocal glasses at the age of seventy-eight.

What will you be doing at seventy? Eighty? Ninety? One hundred? If you give in to the misbelief that there's no use pursuing new goals toward the end of life, you're only hastening the mental decline of your use-it-or-lose-it brain.

Let me make this clear: never say it's too late to change, or it's too late to move forward, or it's too late to learn new things. The words "too late" should repulse you. Never use them. Never let those two words cross your lips. Erase them from your vocabulary. It's *never* too late for you.

I love this story of the famous cellist Pablo Casals. He was ninety-one years old when he was approached by a student who asked, "Master, why do you continue to practice?" Casals replied, "Because I'm making progress."

No matter how old you are, your brain needs oxygen. Exercise brings oxygen to the brain and creates new neurons. Walking, cycling, and other cardiovascular exercises strengthen the heart and the blood vessels that supply the brain with oxygen. Everything that keeps the heart and blood vessels in shape will invigorate the brain. You don't need vigorous exercise to stimulate the growth of new brain neurons. Walking at a brisk pace is sufficient.

Get outside, breathe the fresh air. Don't tell me it's too cold outside. Bundle up and stick your nose out the door. There's a definite correlation between a relationship with nature and your well-being. Stay in touch with nature. If you don't have a garden, buy flowers. If you have allergies, buy nonallergenic plants and take care of them. When they die, buy more. Take a walk every day. Ever notice that after surgery, patients are forced out of bed almost as soon as they're awake to walk the halls toting their IV pole? Walking is good for you! One of my older clients sprints the halls of her apartment building during the winter when it's below zero, and then she flings her front window open and allows the outside air to "clean out the joint," as she puts it. Our brains need oxygen.

The nervous system is divided into two parts. The first part is the central nervous system, which is your brain and spinal cord, the command and control center. The second part is your peripheral nervous system, which brings messages from the sense receptors to the spinal cord and brain, and carries messages from your brain and spinal cord to your muscles and glands.

Your brain needs to be properly and regularly exercised to keep it functioning well. The nucleus basalis, which works by secreting acetylcholine and helps the brain tune in and form sharp memories, has been totally neglected in most older people. In a person with mild cognitive impairment, the acetylcholine produced in the nucleus basalis is not even measurable.[5]

Unlearning can be more difficult than learning, and bad habits are hard to break or unlearn. When we learn a bad habit, it takes over a brain map, and each time we repeat it, it claims more control of that map and prevents the use of that space for good habits. Leading brain plasticity researcher Michael Merzenich believes our neglect of intensive learning as we age leads the systems in the brain that modulate, regulate, and control plasticity to waste away. He claims that a major reason memory loss occurs as we age is that we have trouble registering new events in our nervous system "because processing speed slows down so that the accuracy, strength, and sharpness with which we perceive declines. If you can't register something clearly you won't be able to remember it well."[6]

Look at the brain's life cycle.

Childhood: This is an intense period of learning, and every day brings new experiences and new learning.

Young adulthood: Elementary school, high school, and college bring concentrated learning, and we acquire new skills and abilities. Employment brings new learning, challenges, and skills as well.

Middle age: This is a more placid time of life. We have careers and jobs but rarely engage in tasks in which we must focus our attention as closely as we did when we were younger. Mostly what we engage in now are already learned skills. We have jobs we know how to do, and we do them by rote. We've formed familiar habits for our social life and our downtime. We don't form new stimulating relationships, and if we travel, it's with the same non-involved spectator mentality with which we watch TV. Exercise begins to diminish, and life becomes more laid-back as we prepare for retirement.

Retirement age: Here is where the brain starves for stimulation. Many people in their seventies and older do nothing requiring intense prolonged focus and attention. Physical exercise goes to the wayside, healthy diet choices decline in favor of comfort food, and old habits are stuck to like cement.

If you don't want to get old before your time, give your brain new things to do. Merzenich recommends anything that requires highly focused attention, including learning new physical activities that require concentration. Many physicians tell their older patients to take up learning a new language to improve and maintain their memory and to keep up the production of acetylcholine.

If you do the same physical activity you did thirty years ago as your exercise regime, it won't help your brain's motor cortex stay in shape today. If you're doing the same dances, the same walking routine, the same workout at the gym, you're not keeping your brain alive by learning something new. You need to learn something new with intense focus to lay down new memories and stimulate the brain.

The stress of life, of getting older, releases glucocorticoids, which can kill cells in the brain. But brain science shows that the brain can form new neural pathways. We can add "happy paths" to our brains—at any age! We can recondition our mind-sets. We can end the negative living patterns that we've accepted as okay. We can exercise, get the oxygen flowing to our brains, and teach ourselves the skills of lasting happiness.

Write these words in bold letters in your happiness journal: "Everything that you can see happen in a young brain can happen in an older brain."

Can you teach an old dog new tricks? I don't know about dogs, but according to scientific research, there's no age limit on the ability to learn. When I began teaching How to Be Happy in an Unhappy World workshops, I wasn't sure how older people, especially those set in their ways regarding church, would respond to sitting in Quiet Prayer. I was pleasantly surprised. One man in particular who was in his late eighties loved the teaching I gave on quieting our thoughts, and then when it came time to enter our Quiet Prayer practice, five minutes wasn't long enough. He sat in Quiet Prayer for a half hour, and a fruitful daily practice was launched. It's possible to teach our brains to be happy.

If you like, take five minutes for Quiet Prayer before the next chapter. As you look at God, He is looking at you.

Rest and Idleness
for a Happier You

We have an unspoken notion that busyness equals importance. Our lives can't possibly be without meaning if we're busy. I'm busy, therefore I'm a worthy human being. I'm productive and active and busy, so I count for something. Is all this histrionic exhaustion a way of covering up the fact that most of what we do really doesn't matter? asks Tim Kreider in the *New York Times*. "Idleness is not just a vacation, an indulgence or a vice; it is as indispensable to the brain as vitamin D is to the body, and deprived of it we suffer a mental affliction as disfiguring as rickets," writes Kreider. "The space and quiet that idleness provides is a necessary condition for standing back from life and seeing it whole, for making unexpected connections and waiting for the wild summer lightning strikes of inspiration—it is, paradoxically, necessary to getting any work done."[1]

Think about this for a minute. Consider how hard you worked ten years ago for x-y-z. How important was it really? Does it matter now? I wish I could say that it was truly necessary to nearly kill myself working so hard so many times in the past. We know what we do for Christ is important, but perhaps He doesn't require the same demands we put on ourselves. Happiness depends on knowing when to stop. When to rest. Happiness depends on God's control of our busyness.

Kreider aptly observes that it's not people pulling back-to-back shifts in the ICU or commuting by bus to three minimum-wage jobs who tell you how busy they are. What these people are is not busy but tired. It's almost always people whose lamented busyness is purely self-imposed with work and obligations they've taken on voluntarily. Our own ambition or drive or anxiety often drives us to our addiction to busyness.

Have you noticed that children are busier than ever now? They're scheduled down to the half hour with classes and extracurricular activities. My friend Alice told me, "I have to make an appointment to see my seven-year-old granddaughter between her school, her planned playdates, ballet, flute and art lessons, homework, and cast-in-stone bedtimes. I'm afraid that when she starts adding sports to the schedule I'll be consigned to a seat on the bleachers next to the other grandmas and grandpas with their cameras dangling from their necks." This little girl, just having lost her baby teeth, is as overworked as her parents.

We love to be busy, or maybe we *need* to be busy because we dread what we might have to face if we aren't busy. Do we dread facing ourselves stripped naked of the cloak of our activities? God control of our busyness means taking time to examine His Word for instruction on how to schedule our lives. We need to look at the place rest and idleness have in our daily lives.

Brain Rest

You can tell when your body is tired. You know when your body needs rest from the signs it gives you: slowness, achiness, palpitating heart, headache, swollen feet and ankles, stiff neck, hurting back, stinging eyes. When these symptoms strike, chances are you need to pay attention and get some genuine, cell-restoring rest.

Empirical evidence shows that not only our bodies but also our brains need rest. Our brains are crying for a break from the daily grind of our busy schedules. The benefits of vacation, meditation, time spent outdoors, and napping are necessary to sharpen the mind.

Thomas Aquinas wrote, "It is requisite for the relaxation of the mind that we make use, from time to time, of playful deeds and jokes."[2] This from a thirteenth-century Catholic friar, priest, and saint known as Doctor Angelicus. Deeds and jokes! You'd think he'd be somber and serious with his nose in books all day. He used the word *requisite*, which means necessary, required, essential, indispensable.

Idleness is good for you. Idleness provides space and quietness for you to let go, which is a necessary condition for inspiration. A calm mind is a holy weapon against your challenges. Your brain loves a little peace and quiet.

Salvador Dali's famous melting-clocks painting was inspired during a resting state by a dream. It was this imagery that helped introduce surrealism to the world in the early 1930s. Paul McCartney wrote the iconic song "Yesterday" after receiving the melody in a dream while resting. Orhan Pamuk, the Turkish novelist who won the Nobel Prize in literature in 2006, grew up with a broad imagination and in his grandmother's sitting room pretended he was inside a submarine. Filmmaker Tim Burton daydreamed his way to Hollywood success, spending his childhood alone in his bedroom creating imaginary film posters. Albert Einstein pictured himself running along a light wave—a reverie that led to his theory of relativity.

Relaxing aids in creativity in part because the waking brain never stops working. When relaxing and freeing ourselves of the countless anxieties and worries that besiege us, the mind doesn't slow down or stop working. Neuroscientists have found that calming the mind involves the same brain processes associated with imagination and creativity. Sometimes too much focus on our work can backfire, and our thinking gets in our way. Researchers have found a surprising link between relaxing and creativity. People who relax more are better at generating new ideas.

Experiments conducted on rats revealed a particular pattern of electrical activity in their brains when they were trying to figure their way out of a maze. A period of rest was then given the rats, followed by the same maze challenge. The brains of the rats re-created a nearly identical pattern of electrical impulses moving between the same set of neurons, and they performed better!

Experimental research shows the need for a period of rest following heavy brain exertion. When you give your brain downtime, it replenishes its storehouse of attention and motivation, which encourages productivity and creativity. At rest, the mind is not stuck in time, and we can learn from the past and plan for the future. Moments of quiet and peace are necessary for us to achieve a sense of who we are.

When is the last time you took a nap? (On purpose, I mean—not snoozing while watching TV.) Studies show that taking a nap can sharpen concentration and improve performance on all kinds of tasks, from driving a truck to solving math problems. Taking short breaks while doing brain-taxing work is essential for us to achieve our highest level of performance. A 2004 study analyzed four years of data on highway car accidents involving Italian policemen and concluded that the practice of napping before night shifts reduced the prospective number of collisions by 48 percent.[3]

Neurons in the wake circuit of the brain become fatigued and slow down after many hours of firing during the day. At the time of a nap, the neurons in the sleep circuit speed up and initiate the change to a sleep state. Once someone begins to doze, a short seven to ten minutes of sleep may be enough to restore the wake-circuit neurons to their former excitability.

In a study by Rebecca Smith-Coggins of Stanford University and her colleagues, a group of physicians and nurses who worked three consecutive twelve-hour night shifts were divided into two groups. The first group working the twelve-hour shift stopped to take a forty-minute nap at 3:00 a.m. The other group worked straight through without a nap. The doctors and nurses who napped outperformed the no-nap group on important tests of attention and performance on the job as well as alertness while driving home.[4]

Taking a mental break increases productivity, replenishes attention, solidifies memories, and encourages creativity. Long naps are especially good when people have enough time to recover from post-nap grogginess. In other situations, mini-naps may be a smarter strategy. An intensive 2006 study by Amber Brooks and Leon Lack of Flinders University in Australia tested naps of five, ten, twenty, and thirty minutes to find out which was most restorative. Twenty-four college students periodically slept for only five hours on designated nights. The next day they visited the lab to take their naps. The tests of attention they took required them to respond quickly to images on a screen, complete a word search, and accurately copy sequences of arcane symbols. The five-minute nappers barely increased their alertness after their nap, but those students who napped ten, twenty, and thirty minutes all improved their scores. Ten-minute naps immediately enhanced performance just as much as longer naps without any grogginess.[5] The next time you're hard at work, take a ten-minute nap in your chair to refresh your brain.

Walking is also a restorative and manageable solution to mental fatigue. Try to walk somewhere peaceful—a park, the beach, a wooded area, a quiet neighborhood, or anywhere not peppered with skyscrapers and frantic city streets. Marc Berman, a psychologist at the University of South Carolina and a pioneer of the field called ecopsychology, says that whereas the hustle and bustle of a typical city tax our attention, natural environments restore it.[6]

Contrast the experience of walking through the downtown area of a big city, where the brain is hit with loud noise, chaos, honking taxies, and crowds of strangers, with a hike in a nature reserve, where the mind is free to leisurely shift its focus from the calls of birds to the sound of the wind to the sunlight falling through every gap in the tree branches.

In one controlled ecopsychology experiment by Dr. Berman, he asked thirty-eight University of Michigan students to study lists of random numbers and recite them from memory in reverse order. When they finished, he had them complete another attention-draining task in which they memorized the locations of certain words arranged in a grid. Afterward, he sent half the students for a stroll along a shady tree-strewn path in an arboretum for an hour. The other half walked the same distance through highly trafficked streets of downtown Ann Arbor for the same period of time.

Back at the lab, the students were given one more test memorizing and reciting digits. The students who ambled among trees were able to recall 1.5 more digits than they had during the first test. Those who walked through the city improved by only 0.5 digits. Downtime can bulk up the muscle of attention in the brain.

Rest and Happiness

Happy people need rest. Relaxation and leisure are necessary components of leading a happy life, not only because of the pleasure they provide but also because the brain requires them. You can't be the happiest person or the best person you were meant to be without rest. The importance of leisure has been well known for centuries. The Roman poet Ovid wrote in 23 BC, "In our leisure we reveal what kind of people we are."[7]

How to be happy in an unhappy world includes knowing how to rest, how to nap, how to take a leisurely walk in the middle of your average workday. Breathe the air, count the stars, dance on the grass, sing in the shower, listen to music, hike in the woods, walk in silence, tell a funny story, kiss someone on the cheek. Be glad for the relief of laughter and relaxation. Give your brain the freedom it needs to carry on its best work. Give your body the calmness it craves. In our leisure, if taken with intention, we can really discover who we are. It's here we can construct the true fabric of our beings. Stress-free and open, we are free to simply be.

Best of all, pull yourself aside from the daily routine, sit yourself down, close your eyes, and get alone with God. Step aside from everything going on around you—your work, concerns, worries, efforts, thoughts, plans, deadlines, pressures—and simply allow yourself to be alone in God's presence. Bring a quality of holy awareness to the moment. I've never seen anyone stress out after a Quiet Prayer. In five to twenty minutes, you can go from anxious to calm without drugs, alcohol, or another person to talk you out of your mood. You do it yourself by focusing your mind and your body in the presence of God. One moment of awareness, one breath when you are truly present, can be quite profound. See for yourself!

I was walking on a downtown street of the small beach town where I live when I saw a little clothing shop I'd never seen before. I immediately popped inside thinking it had just opened, and the salesperson said they'd been there ten years! I had walked past it maybe a hundred times and had never seen it. I felt so guilty I bought a hat. Talking about it later with a friend, I realized I had noticed the shop because Quiet Prayer and holy awareness had made me more aware in my everyday life.

The more you practice awareness, the more you'll begin to notice more of the world around you with open spiritual eyes. You'll discover that you've become more spiritually aware. You can expect to be able to hear from God in subtle ways that you may not have been able to hear before. You'll observe more things, including more painful things. When you begin to observe the painful things, you'll find it easier to face them without fear or turning away. The Holy Spirit opens the gates of understanding and compassion within you.

When we learn to stop complaining about bad situations or about pain and start embracing understanding and compassion, we realize we can know pain as completely and fully as we know any other experience. We need not fear pain.

Be careful not to try too hard when practicing stillness. Don't try to make anything happen or to achieve any special effects. Simply relax and pay as much attention as you can to what is present, whatever form that takes. Allow yourself to experience life as it unfolds, paying careful and openhearted attention to the moment.

The physical benefits of Quiet Prayer include lower blood pressure; lower levels of blood lactate; reduced anxiety attacks; a decrease of tension-related pain, such as tension headaches; a disappearance of ulcers, insomnia, and muscle and joint problems; an increase in serotonin production, which improves mood and behavior; an improved immune system; and increased physical energy levels.

The mental benefits of Quiet Prayer include increased emotional stability, creativity, and intuition; mental clarity; sharpening of the mind; and the diminishing of problems.

Quiet Prayer increases the volume and density of the memory area of the brain. It thickens regions of the frontal cortex that control our emotions, and it delays the typical wilting of brain areas responsible for sustaining attention as we get older. Over time, you may also develop a more intricately wrinkled cortex, the brain's outer layer, which is necessary for sophisticated mental abilities, such as abstract thought and introspection.

As you know by now, how to be happy in an unhappy world places premium importance on holy awareness and attentiveness. True and lasting happiness depends on being aware, mindful, and conscious. Self-awareness is the first step in this journey. It is crucial that you be aware of yourself and who you are in Christ. Be conscious of yourself in the loving arms of God and how you live as His beloved.

One definition of rest I like is "to stop something so it can be made strong again." To be strong in the world and in our lives, we must also speak words that build up, inspire, and strengthen us. Speak powerful, uplifting words when you're at rest because you can rob your brain and your body of the rest they crave by your complaints. "I'm so tired!" "I work so hard!" "If I don't do it, it won't get done!" "I'm always on a killer deadline!" "I can't get off the treadmill!" "Nobody appreciates how hard I work!" "I don't get paid enough for the work I do!" "I'm taken advantage of in this thankless job!" "I'm so stressed out!" "Work is just one big pressure machine, and I'm caught in it!" "This is killing me!"

Your body is listening to what you say. The body stores emotional memories. These statements can lock your brain and body in a stressed-out prison. The pathways of the brain remain in stressed-out ruts with no relief, and your body will begin to act out its unhappiness in its own various manners of pain and malfunction.

Change your self-talk. "Ah, rest! I love it!" "I love to relax and take time to be grateful." "This time of leisure is beautiful!" "I'm so happy to be able to rest and reflect on the blessings of God in my life!"

My artist friend Pacia Dixon, who lives in Washington State, sent this email to me in California after we had both gotten home from being on a women's retreat together. It expresses what I'm talking about here:

Dear Marie,

Things here are going well as I adjust to life at home. Monday I managed to unpack my suitcase and straighten up the house. But then, when I went out to the deck to sweep away the fallen maple leaves and their "helicopters," I came across an amber leaf with what looked like a henna tattoo. When I held it up against the sunshine, it glowed like a stained glass window. What could I do but drop the broom and dance?

Solitude

Dance your love for God. And then consider another form of refreshing, which is to withdraw for a time of solitude.

The first chapter of Mark tells us that after Jesus ministered and taught all day, He went to the home of Simon (Peter) and Andrew and healed Peter's mother-in-law. It was a full and demanding day for Jesus, the kind of day you come home from and just want to eat dinner, jump into a hot bath, go to bed, and sleep ten hours. But then verse 32 says, that evening "they brought to Him all who were sick and those who were demon-possessed," and the whole city was gathered together at the door. Considering the crowd, Jesus must have worked long into the night praying and healing person after person. He had to have been tired. However, in verse 35, Mark tells us, "Now in the morning, having risen a long while before daylight, He went out and departed to a solitary place; and there He prayed."

Before daylight.

He probably slept only two or three hours at most. To Jesus, being alone with God was more important than sleep. He needed more than physical refreshment; He needed to be refreshed spiritually. So He departed to a solitary place, having risen "a long while before daylight." He left the house and went out in the dark to a secluded place to pray.

When you look at your relationship with God, how much time do you spend alone with Him?

When I was a young girl in New York as a dancer and actor, I carried a Bible with every verse circled that indicated I could get what I wanted. When I went to an audition, I pulled out verses to assure myself I'd land the job. I was a Christian, but I saw God as somewhere out there in the cosmos with all the answers to my prayers, and my job was to get Him to hear me and help me. I believed in Jesus, but my religion was dance. My dedication was all consuming. My prayers and my life as a believer were centered on me and my work. It never dawned on me to withdraw from everything for a time and be alone with God. Wasn't that something only nuns did?

Today the more I read that passage in Mark that says Jesus "departed to a solitary place," the more I realize how desperately all of us need to pull away at times from the pursuits and demands of daily life to enter a secluded, solitary place with God.

I believe it's when we're alone with God that we learn best who He is. You can read, study, pray, sing, dance, and worship, but being alone with Him, hanging out with Him and His Word for long periods of time, is the most amazing, revelatory experience you can have. Being with Him without rushing away to do your own thing, being with Him with no clock at your side, being with Him to learn how to love the way He loves—there's nothing like it.

Just because you're active in some form of ministry doesn't mean you're automatically close to God. Our busyness for God can take the place of our closeness to Him.

In my book *Angels in Our Lives*, I tell about the extended time I spent alone with God when He drew me out of the world to be set apart and alone with Him. I felt in my heart that I was being called away for a time just to be alone with the Lord. My ministry and speaking engagements were put on hold. I was busy teaching and writing in the academic world, and I thought everything was just fine. I thought I was being a blessing. But I obeyed and did what I heard Him telling me to do and just quietly closed up shop. It was sort of like dying. I was still at home, and I still had family and certain obligations, but my normal life came to a stop. I was a hermit of sorts, unnoticed, irrelevant, extremely poor, and oddly enough, content.

Every day I hiked the woods with God as my partner. In my isolated time with the Lord, He showed me that the broken and surrendered life is the highest calling on earth. Each day as I experienced more of Him, I felt more of me break off. There were areas in my life where pain had been my teacher and not the Holy Spirit. The things that can fuel a demanding life, like pride and ambition, shattered around my feet. As I submerged myself in His Word and spent my days with Him, I felt my entire life disintegrate to then bloom again.

Henri Nouwen had a way of looking at solitude. He said solitude is "the furnace of transformation" and "the place where the old self dies and the new self is born, the place where the emergence of the new man and the new woman occurs."[8]

Without God at the core and center of our lives, our identity is fabricated by social compulsions and the need for ongoing and increasing affirmation. Thomas Merton calls this the secular or the false self.[9] "Who am I?" we ask, and the false self's answer is reliant on how we're perceived by the world. If being busy is a good thing, then I must be busy. If being beautiful gives me favor, I must be beautiful. If having money is a sign of freedom, then I must get money. If knowing important people makes me important, I must pursue and make necessary contacts. Do you see the traps that we set in front of us?

Happiness dangles at the tip of the string of our worldly dependencies. When your sense of self depends on achieving goals set by culture, you'll never know real happiness. It's not possible.

In solitude, we empty ourselves of the misconceptions that have held us bound to fits of unhappiness. In solitude, without the distractions of the outside world, without the noise and clamor of pursuits and goals, we can detach ourselves from our neurotic needs and demands and put our empty souls into the open arms of God to allow Him to fill us with Himself.

Divine presence within you is discovered, nurtured, and cherished most in solitude. "The Divine Presence is not a distant goal toward which one must perennially labor like some haunted Sisyphus," writes contemporary author John O'Donohue. "There is nothing nearer to us than the divine; we need only slip into rhythm with it."[10]

How often should you head off to be alone with the Lord? And for how long? That's strictly up to you and the Lord. I withdraw as often as I can, and I can't use my demanding schedule as an excuse because my Benedictine brothers and sisters withdraw six times a day, and their schedules are no less demanding than mine. You can take yourself off for a weekend retreat to be with the Lord alone, or you can go for long daily walks with Him wherever you live. If you're in a busy city with its many distractions, you might want to withdraw into an empty room or simply turn off your cellphone, TV, and all electronics. Put aside all outside interferences and enter a period of solitude right where you are.

Getting alone with God is like being invited to a royal ball. First, you get yourself ready. You take extra care bathing and showering, you wear your best clothes, you make sure you look your best, and with the personal invitation to the ball tucked in your sleeve, you head for the ball. That's what getting ready to be alone with God is like. Bathing is repentance. Getting dressed is taking off your regular everyday lifestyle to party with Him by special invitation.

A great way to learn about repentance and forgiveness is to accept the invitation to spend time alone with Jesus. There are so many avenues leading to repentance and forgiveness, and your task is to find the avenue that leads to your personal freedom from anything that separates you from your better self and your freedom in Christ. The unrepentant soul is an unhappy soul. Always preface your prayers with the knowledge of your human state, and confess what you know you need to confess. Ask for forgiveness and then relax. You're forgiven.

We know that we fall short of the glory of God, but don't let sin keep you from Him. Don't let shame stick its nose in your business. When Jesus forgives, He says, "Go, and sin no more." Beautiful words. Be unburdened, guiltless, and free. Confess and be free. "If we confess our sins, He is faithful and just to forgive us our sins and to cleanse us from all unrighteousness" (1 John 1:9). Our sins and lawless acts He will remember no more (Heb. 10:17).

If we're half as smart as we think we are, we'll recognize we don't do life well on our own. The smarter we get, the more we can see that the needs, hopes, dreams, and desires we've clung to sink us faster than pockets full of stones. Open yourself to God's goals, desires, dreams, and hopes. These are what He waits to give you. Empty yourself of pride, envy, greed, sloth, gluttony, lust, and anger (the seven deadly sins). He paid for all your sins and mistakes, even the spiritual ones.

St. Augustine said that God's most faithful servant's first and greatest aim is to hear what is most pleasing to God. Here's a happiness journal assignment: Ask yourself if you know what is most pleasing to God. Can you give it to Him? When will you do it?

It doesn't matter so much what you do in life or what kinds of works are yours. What matters is the ground on which your works are built. The "ground" is who you are. If you're honest, your works will be grounded in honesty. If you're wise, your works will be grounded in wisdom. Think of every act you do as holy. Eating, sleeping, sweeping the floor, shopping, taking the dog for a walk—all holy acts. What you do can't be holy if *you* aren't holy, and your holiness is born out of becoming one with the divine presence of God in you. If there were a better form of living, He would have told us so.

Imagine Jesus standing next to you right where you are now. Imagine Him speaking these words to you:

> Your spiritual strength and wisdom
> are born in the quiet place with Me.
>   Allow your thoughts and your many needs
> and worries today to hush in the Presence of Perfection.
>   I am your God.
> Your peace of mind is here with Me in the quiet place
>   where I wait for you daily.
> I will create a new heart in you as you lean into Mine,
>   waiting and listening. Let Me comfort you
> and stroke your brow. In the multitude of your anxieties
>   My comforts will delight your soul.

The whirlwind of your daily life can leave you
    wind-swept and disheveled, but here with Me,
you are the portraiture of serenity and calm.
    I speak peace to you, to your home and
all that you possess. When your heart is at peace, you
      bring
    peace to everything around you.[11]

The Beautiful Now

We lock ourselves in a pattern of unhappiness by compromising with darkness. We may not know it, but we're asleep in the light. "Dress yourselves in Christ, and be up and about!" the Message says in Romans 13:14. When we're caught up in ourselves, we can't see clearly. We can't see things as they are.

Seeing Things as They Are

I was once in a taxi with a glamorous celebrity on our way to a promotional dinner when she broke a fingernail. You would have thought Vesuvius had erupted over Pompeii. She refused to go to the dinner with a broken fingernail, so we had no choice but to go to the dinner without her. There were no nail salons open to have it fixed, so she went back home. When I spoke with her the next day, I told her about the evening she missed, but she couldn't have cared less. What mattered was her manicure.

A broken fingernail, a broken car, a broken computer, a broken body—you name it—they are all part of the fabric of life with the potential to strengthen us and bring us blessings or waste our time and rob us of happiness. You come to a deep hole in the road, and you either jump in or walk around it. Obsessing over the problem is one response that will cause you to miss more than a nice dinner. You're your own problem. The circumstances are incidental.

The words you flood your brain with are like bulldozers in clay. They form deep ruts, and if they're negative, pathetic words of defeat, you're the reason for your unhappiness. You've accepted and owned negativity as yours.

When negative things occur in your life, like the computer crashes, the car suddenly needs a new battery and a fan belt, a friend betrays you, the kids get the chicken pox when you're going on vacation, your spouse loses a job opportunity, your hairdresser moves to Cancún, what do you do? I'll give you three ways you can handle the situation.

The first is to fall apart emotionally and obsess over it, get on the phone and tell all the people you can every detail, and generally make yourself upset, stressed, and depressed. All because you grabbed the problem and embraced it by your perception of its negative power in your life.

Life doesn't make you unhappy. You make yourself unhappy. Circumstances don't stress you out. You stress yourself out.

The second way to handle the unwanted situations we face in life is to fight them. We put on our feeble battle helmets and come out swinging.

You can spend your life fighting back in your human strength and never enter lasting happiness or the sweet peace and joy you were meant to have in the Spirit. You can get so carried away retaliating, fighting back, and settling the score that you forget how to mellow out and proclaim God's guidance and justice in the matter. You're so uptight, with both fists punching the air, that you can't relax in the expansive cushion of God's sweet, delicious love and

His perfect guidance. You forget how to sit down and have a good laugh over it all. Miracles and help from God don't require your emotional tornadoes. God doesn't need blasts of righteous fury to act on your behalf. He's good with simple trust.

When you're wronged, it's easy to take the low road and fight back, return a wrong for a wrong, and feed on bitter anger: "I'll show them!" "Nobody does that to me!" "I have my rights!" Let me say this to you: miracles happen when you let go.

Return to and hold tight the promises of the Lord: "'No weapon formed against you shall prosper, and every tongue which rises against you in judgment you shall condemn. This is the heritage of the servants of the LORD, and their righteousness is from Me,' says the Lord" (Isa. 54:17).

When you're in a stressful, all-hands-on-deck, panic situation, the third and best method is to immediately run to the place inside where the Spirit of God has fused with your human spirit. Let the softness of His breath and the excitement of the challenge sweep over you. Allow yourself to soften in His presence. You do this by pausing, taking a breath, observing the unwanted situation, and then accepting it for what it is, even if it's painful. Don't deny, avoid, or obsess over the painful thing that's happened to you. And let go of the urge to deal with it emotionally or to fight back instantly. Allow yourself to "be" with the experience. You are getting in touch with who you are, and the experience just happens to be there too.

This is an exercise that takes effort and concentration on your part. Think of your experience, whatever it is, as a challenge designed to open up what's inside you. Once you accept the unalterable fact that God is with you and in you, you can begin to accept the challenge as a joint one, yours and His. "He who is in you is greater than your own natural, self-centered, frantic self," to paraphrase 1 John 4:4.

Next, begin to let go of the tension you're feeling. Just let it go. You can do this anywhere. Release the tension in your body by simply taking some deep breaths. Try breathing from the dia-phragm, not your chest. Don't hunch up your shoulders as you breathe in. Allow your shoulders to relax.

Most of us are not aware of the spiritual dimension inside us. If we were, we wouldn't so easily panic when things go wrong. Paus-ing to breathe is a great tool. One experience comes to mind when I was preaching in a little church in Bemidji, Minnesota, and the electricity went out in the middle of the service. I paused, breathed deeply, and then rather than sending everyone home, I preached for thirty more minutes in the pitch dark! We had a wonderful time, and the Lord gave me a terrific message (it ministered to me, anyhow) about the benefits and blessings of darkness.

Can you see the benefits of darkness? Can you see the glory in the unknown, the mystery, the challenge? You will never be happy if you remain afraid of the dark. "There is no such thing as dark-ness," said one Quiet Prayer respondent, "only a failure to see."

So there you are, you now have

- observed the situation
- accepted the situation
- allowed yourself to "be" within the experience of the situation
- released all tension from your body
- allowed yourself to be at peace

"Peace I give to you; not as the world gives do I give to you," Jesus said (John 14:27); so now, at this moment of letting go, you relinquish your expectations of the world to give you peace.

I may feel better when the car is fixed, the kids are healthy, the bills are paid, and the people I care about care about me, but real peace and joy come from inside me, that place of light where God lives.

When you're upset, angry, hurt, depressed, or anxious, remind yourself that it's not the situation that is important but what you tell yourself about the situation. Knowing and listening to what you tell yourself are key to your lasting happiness. You can be surrounded by blessings and not know it.

It's What's Inside That Counts

You're a success in life when you find your personhood in God. Then you don't have to care what anybody thinks about you or what anybody says about you. You're able to look out from the windows of your heart and see the world around you for what it is. You stop expecting the world to take care of you.

If you change your profession, you may be doing something different that makes you feel better, but it doesn't change who you are. If you change your clothes tonight, you're still the same person inside. If you change your hairstyle, lose an arm, or get old, you haven't changed who you are. This is what you have to understand. Your outward efforts to feel better, to live a satisfied, happy life, will enhance your inner sense of well-being momentarily, but the feelings won't last. Nothing in this world is permanent. Only God is permanent. Hook up with Him if you want permanent. Instead of spending your time changing your situations and relationships, change what's inside you.

The fundamental key to lasting happiness and the purpose of this book is to help you get to the place where you're at peace with who you are, when you can say, as Anthony De Mello quips, "Though everything is a mess, all is well."[1]

True happiness is not caused. You can't make me happy. You, my work, my home, my friends, my ministry aren't my happiness. The me who takes part in these is where my true, lasting happiness lives. Inside, not outside. Events and situations can change happy feelings to unhappy feelings in a minute. You receive a phone call with bad news or you realize someone you thought was a friend is just out to use you—and out the door go your feelings of happiness.

Let me tell you about an experience I had not that long ago. I received a traffic ticket for going through a red light (I was sure it was yellow), and when I saw the bill, I went crazy. That traffic ticket ($600.00!) in my hand was a wake-up call for me. I knew my emotional reaction didn't have to do with the ticket itself. The ticket was not the issue. The issue was where my response came from and the misbelief I held regarding the ticket. I sat down with the ticket in my hand, and I saw the misbelief: "I shouldn't have to pay for my mistakes."

The situation wasn't about the $600.00 I couldn't afford, or the traffic cop who stopped me, or the San Diego Police Department, or my car, or my busy life, or the weather, or the yellow light. It was about me and my misbelief.

We spend our lives trying to change what's around us when it's ourselves that need changing. We get into relationships and waste years trying to change the other guy when we have no idea who *we* are. Reality is what is in you. Negative and positive feelings are in you.

Exploring What's Good

As you read this book, eighty to one hundred billion neurons are signaling one another in a network of synapse connections in your brain. New synapses will start growing within minutes depending on what you feed them. We grow new neural circuits in our brains when we replace our negative thinking with positive thoughts. The brain is wonderfully flexible and teachable. You can teach your brain the skills of happiness!

Your experiences matter, and how you allow them to carve space in your brain is up to you. Love, worry, and anger can each make changes in your neural networks. If you continually criticize yourself, stress out over what others say or do, find fault with the way things are going, or tell yourself life is unfair, your brain will become negative. Instead, tell yourself the truth as God sees the truth with statements such as, "This situation isn't the best, but through Christ I can handle it," "Though I didn't choose this to happen, I am okay," "Life is good in spite of this," "God is on the throne, and it is well with my soul," "Surely goodness and mercy are following me all the days of my life." What you pay attention to and fix your mind on shape the patterns in your brain.

Telling yourself the truth takes effort. It takes turning from your complaints, woes, miseries, and feelings of anger. It means letting it all go. After you let go, begin to tell yourself lovely things. It's time to take charge of how your brain is being shaped.

Look at the smallest things in life that make you happy. I asked a depressed client I'll call Betty to describe for me the feeling she got when she felt an autumn wind in her hair. She drew a blank. I asked her to describe for me the taste of her favorite food, chocolate. I asked her to tell me one happy thing that had happened to her that day before she came to see me. "Nothing," she said. "Nothing good ever happens to me." I waited. Then her eyes widened. "Well, actually . . ." she began with wonder in her voice. Then she told me how her twenty-one-year-old son had taken her for a ride on his motorcycle that morning, and when they were almost home, he had shouted back at her that he loved her. "Isn't that beautiful?" she said, her voice trembling. "Isn't that *beautiful?*"

Because she wasn't accustomed to connecting with the "beautiful now," Betty wasn't aware that she had felt genuinely happy that morning. She was so trained in negativity that she needed to learn to give herself permission to be present, aware, and happy. It took a lot of work, but her words that day, "Isn't that beautiful?" were a tremendous breakthrough on her happiness journey.

What beautiful things have happened to you today (besides spending time with me reading this book)?

Take some time before you go to sleep to write down the good, happy things you observed and experienced in your day. Live those moments fully as you write them down. I always feel so blessed as a writer because I get to experience good things twice: once at the moment I experience them, and again through writing about them.

Today I am grateful for
  1.
  2.
  3.

Today God showed me the following beautiful truths:
  1.
  2.
  3.

Today I felt happy when
  1.
  2.
  3.

In this organized way, your happiness journal will fill up with the blessings you might have missed if you weren't consciously aware of finding and recording them.

A young, distraught man told me, "I've been negative my entire life. It cost me my marriage." I helped him begin to look for and find good things going on around him and in the world each day. It was no easy task for him. He said he felt stupid looking for good things to be happy about when the world was going to hell in a handbasket. It took a few weeks, but then he told me, "I feel like I'm ferreting out the good in life. I kinda like it."

He listed some of his ferreting: "The Lakers won last night." "I walked to work and it felt good." "I had a great conversation with my daughter." "I realized how much I enjoy the smell of Italian food cooking."

King Solomon in the Bible wrote 1,005 songs (1 Kings 4:32), and the Song of Songs is considered his finest. In the Hebrew language, it's the highest of the highest. It shows us that at the center of us there's a voice. That voice is calling to us and telling us everything we need to hear: you are Mine and I am yours. The voice of the Lover of our souls calls to us to come away with Him; the time is now, the beautiful now.

Seeing God as He is takes spiritual eyes, and you need the Holy Spirit to see with spiritual eyes. You need spiritual ears to hear His voice. Song of Songs 4:9 says, "You have ravished my heart with one look of your eyes." You're the beloved. And Jesus is telling you He's ravished by one look from your fabulous eyes. And this powerful, ecstatic exchange of looks catapults you into His presence. Zing! There you are! Can you absorb this? Can you see you're beautiful now?

When God looks across all the earth, He sees only one thing pure in all of creation: His chosen ones, you. You are the pure thing God looks for and loves. Mike Bickle writes, "When your deepest truth is that you are the Beloved of God, and when your greatest joy comes from fully claiming that truth, it follows that this has to become visible and tangible in the ways you eat and drink, talk and love, play and work."[2]

You don't belong to the world. And this is precisely why you're sent into the world. Your presence moving through the dark shadows of the world with the Lover of your soul permits the world a glimpse of real life and real happiness.

I've seen the great Rio Grande dried up, a dusty rut in a landscape of cracked and fissured sand. It makes the heart sick. God is calling you, beloved river, to bubble up, flow, and thrive. In the midst of painful reality, you have to dare to claim the truth that you're God's beloved one even when the world doesn't choose you. It's time to grow up in your beautiful now and flow toward who you're called to be.

Three Stages of Your Renewed Life

Let's take a look at the stages of growth we go through as Christians.[3] To live dominated by the Spirit of God is a process. It's not a single event. Think of this in three stages. One spiritual level moves you to another. How long you spend in each level of growth is up to you.

Stage 1

Here's where we conform. It's a good stage. This is where we learn to trade the old for the new. This is a repenting, turning stage that's like spending a week in the shower. The Ten Commandments often dominate us in this phase. Being spiritual in this phase depends on keeping a list of dos and don'ts, on keeping the rules—whatever they are—and doing everything right. The river may have little current here, and the surface is either placid or passionate with emotion.

Stage 1 is when we're introduced to amazing grace, and some people stay at this point of their new birth and don't grow from here. In stage 1, we grasp that we're saved from past deadly choices and every sin that disabled and dishonored us (Eph. 2:8) and that amazing grace is our inheritance.

A problem can occur in stage 1 if we're working so desperately at doing the right thing to please God that we can't recognize His joyous side. We want to do everything right, and we can even see ourselves as superior somehow, better than people who don't believe as we do or work as hard as we do. The stage 1 believer needs to understand that to be born again in Christ is freedom. In stage 1, we can be very legalistic.

Sadly, some people stay in this stage for their entire Christian walk. These are the ones who put people down if they don't fit with their particular mode of faith. I have a friend who has stayed in stage 1 for years. He just never goes any further than seeing God as a force up in the sky heaping rules and restrictions on His people. You can tell how unhappy he is by the way he hammers and pounds at life and the world with his Bible. He's not led by love and therefore can't seem to move on to stage 2.

When an entire community of believers stays locked in stage 1, obsessed with religious rules and regulations, the living presence of the Holy Spirit is kept at bay. Unfortunately, it's the stage 1 judgmental, stiff-necked, Bible-thumping church that the world judges all Christians by. One morning I started a conversation with a woman standing outside a New Age church selling books at a book table. I told her I was a Christian and that I went to such-and-such church. She looked at me with great pity in her eyes. "Oh, honey," she said, as though I'd lost a leg or something, "I am so sorry." She felt sorry for me! She felt sorry for me because I was a Christian! What did she think we were?

Stage 2

Stage 2 is inspired realization. This is an exciting and productive stage. The Bible really starts to come alive to the stage 2 believer. The stage 2 level of the spiritual life has more to do with *becoming* than it does with trying to look good by doing the right thing. We're ready to set out to become the kind of people we were put on earth to be. Most evangelical Christians live in this level of faith. Committed, involved, and interested in promoting the work of God, the stage 2 believer is no longer an observer of the Word. They are a doer of the Word. Christian missions, schools, hospitals, universities, human rights organizations, food distribution, orphanages, disaster relief, prayer rooms, free clinics, and more are initiated, founded, and funded by predominantly stage 2 believers.

Once in stage 2, we begin to move deeper into a realization of what's happening to us and in us by God's Spirit. Letting go, loving God, and seeing more of His big picture take place at this stage. Holiness now isn't a hammer over our heads; it's a privilege. It's the life of the Holy Spirit within us really taking root. In this stage, we can fall in love with the Word of God, joyfully cling to the promises of God and the beautiful hope He gives us. We begin to grasp the gifts and fruit of the Holy Spirit. We know God is calling us to a deeper walk in Him, and we joyfully follow where He leads even though the road ahead may be rocky and even if we don't completely understand where He's leading us.

We begin to drop our prejudices in this stage. We stop judging other Christians if they're not like us, and we develop a deep love for the world as we see it through the loving eyes of God. We become warmer people, happier and better adjusted to pain as well as to joy. Stage 2 is a continual state of discovery. Everything is new, amazing, exciting. At least it should be.

Some powerful evangelists come forth in these first two levels. Some of them haven't known the Lord very intimately and their river doesn't run very deep, but their zeal is infectious, and God uses them to crack open hardened hearts.

Stage 3

In stage 3, we roll up our sleeves and act with amazing feats of faith. We have put on the mind of Christ. We give ourselves openly and completely to be filled with and led by the Holy Spirit.

It's in this level where no division in the faith exists. There are no denominational barriers. We love, honor, and are one with all churches, denominations, and fellowships who lift up the name of Jesus as Savior. We don't look for fault and seek only to find goodness and love in a brother or sister and their faith. Love possesses us, and there's no task too large or small that God cannot ask of us.

The level of intimacy with the Beloved at this stage is intense and glorious. Here's where we find and keep happiness solidly alive in our inner being, and we let nothing rip it from us. In this level, we have no need to plead or beg God. Peace that passes understanding (Phil. 4:7) overtakes us. We're being transformed day by day and learning to truly know God from the inside out. We begin to see how liberating it is never to feel the urge to ask why of God. The joy of the Lord has become our strength (Neh. 8:10). Here is where our souls soar and our spirits take wing with the Holy Spirit having reign over our thoughts, choices, actions, plans, needs, and desires. In stage 3, we learn transforming miracles that change us into His image, like the beloved one in Song of Songs. We carry the mind of Christ into our everyday lives.

You'll find most of God's monastic and contemplative Christians at this level because it's such an intense level of *internal* dedication. It's here where works are the fruit of a rich inner life. Stage 3 believers don't fake anything. What you see is what you get.

In this level, we join hearts with our spiritual mothers and fathers and the precious martyrs, saints, and heroes of the faith who've gone before us. Stage 3 believers are the present-day martyrs we hear about in the world—men, women, and children who bravely endure unspeakable persecution and lay down their lives for Christ. They are the light of the world.

It's at stage 1 that a person usually falls from the faith. Stage 2 and 3 believers may sin and take a downward tumble, but they don't usually leave the faith. Stage 1 believers, because they're at their weakest, are the ones who might throw in the towel and buy into the world's lie that there's something better out there. Stage 2 and 3 believers know better. They may shame God and themselves, but they don't leave Him. In time, they come back restored.

At each stage of growth, Jesus in us is a life in the beautiful now, alive and pulsing, like a river of living water. Everywhere we go we bring His presence. Every once in a while, I'll have this astonishing experience in which a stranger will come up to me and say something like, "I see something special in you! Who are you?" Once I was in a shopping mall and a woman rushed across the aisle to me and exclaimed, "I see God in you!" (I was stunned. I wasn't even thinking about God. I was thinking about how much that dress on the mannequin cost.) Another time I was on a Hollywood TV set on a writing assignment, and when I walked in, an actor jumped up with his finger pointed at my face and said, "You're one of them, aren't you? You're a Christian!"

I'm telling you this because you just never know what people see when you show up. Everywhere you place your foot you bring God. What would happen if we began looking for God in each other? What would it be like to actually expect and recognize the light on a hill in each other?

Here's a happiness journal exercise. Think of one to five people you know in whom you can see God's light. Write down their names and how you're going to express your appreciation to them.

All religions and philosophies hunger for Jesus whether they know it or not. Jesus is everything we all ache for. He is the joy of man's desire. Stage 1 believers aren't always aware of the greatness of the Holy Spirit in them. They know God is a Trinity—Father, Son, and Holy Spirit—but it ends there. It's important for you to know that the light within I'm talking about is Jesus Himself as the person of the Holy Spirit. What's inside you is dazzling with happiness.

If you like, pause and take five minutes to nurture and develop your happiness quotient with Quiet Prayer before going on to the final chapter.

The Happiness Recovery Plan

Not long ago, we had a conversation in my living room with Nan, a delightful seventy-year-old Christian lady who had traveled from out of town to take part in Quiet Prayer with a group of us. She had a vibrancy about her, and so naturally I asked her what made her such a happy person.

She said, "You know, Marie, it's funny. When you get to be my age and you look back on the past, you see how much time you wasted being concerned about things that really didn't matter at all. Here I am, seventy years old, and it really doesn't matter that my son left the bathroom light on when he was a child, or that my husband didn't take out the garbage, or that I spent too much money on my hair, or that grape juice was spilled on the carpet twenty-five years ago. I remember getting so upset over things that really were inconsequential in the total scheme of things. Now I know that what really matters is loving God with a pure heart and loving life and people with that same love."

Her eyes sparkled as she went on. "It feels wonderful to be free now of all the stupid things I was so concerned with all my life.

I've gotten wise, I guess. And I've learned that the wisest thing a person can do is to cherish where they are at in the moment. I'm wiser now, and I'm cherishing my life now exactly as it is."

What makes her story so inspiring is that Nan had Stage 4 cancer.

The French author Colette exclaimed when she was eighty years old, "What a wonderful life I've had! I only wish I'd realized it sooner!"[1]

The Austrian psychiatrist W. Beran Wolfe, born in 1900, gave us this wisdom: "If you observe a really happy man you will find him building a boat, writing a symphony, educating his son, growing double dahlias in his garden, or looking for dinosaur eggs in the Gobi desert. He will not be searching for happiness as if it were a gold button that has rolled under the cupboard. . . . He will have become aware that he is happy in the course of living life twenty-four crowded hours of the day."[2]

Yet as we've learned, lasting happiness exists even in the face of suffering and difficulties.

Happiness in Spite of Suffering

Saint Faustina, the Polish nun who authored the *Chaplet of Divine Mercy*, said, "There are two things angels envy us humans for. One is the Eucharist [Communion] and the other is suffering."[3] This is an astounding statement and one that prompts us to honor our suffering instead of letting it terrify us. How many hospital rooms do I enter to pray for people where the walls are coated with panic, fear, and shame? "I shouldn't be here." "Why hasn't God healed me?" "What's going to happen to me?" "Is this my fault?" "I don't want to die." "Get me out of here." "Where is God?" "Why is this happening to me?"

The apostle Paul taught us to suffer with dignity: "I know whom I have believed and am persuaded that He is able to keep what I have committed to Him until that Day" (2 Tim. 1:12).

I've prayed for people whose panic exceeded their malady. Emotional pain screams for the Lord's loving touch. When His peace that passes human comprehension enters the sickroom, it's like spring blossoming forth from frozen panes of ice. I've remembered for a long time something said by William Faulkner: "If I were to choose between pain and nothing, I would choose pain."[4]

What is important is not what happens to you; it's what you do with what happens to you. Worry, fear, and intense self-concern are self-destructive activities to your body, soul, and spirit. The longer you dwell on your misfortunes, the greater is their power over you. You're not the illness or the problem. You're God's partner in managing it.

How much thought and effort you give to becoming a happy person is up to you. Can you name three ways you'll make yourself happy every day?

Dr. Alfred Adler, who founded the School of Individual Psychology, claimed that it's the person who's not interested in his fellow man who has the greatest difficulties in life and provides the greatest injuries to others.

When are we the least interested in our fellow man? Answer: when we're hurting. The big difference between being happy and being unhappy is that when we feel unhappy, we're concerned mainly with ourselves, excluding all else. When we're hurting, we feel nobody else could possibly suffer this badly, and if they are, so what.

When I've been broken apart inside, I've had to force myself to give to someone else, even if the tears were still stinging my cheeks. There's a saying I cherish and tell myself often: "A bit of fragrance always clings to the hand that gives roses."

I believe we can all be rose givers in our unique ways. But it's difficult to reach out to help another person when our own life is in the pits. I know. If you're a victim of burnout or in the throes of falling apart, your thoughts are directed at yourself. Forget the world. When we're depressed or anxious, we don't think clearly at all.

The big struggle we face is between choosing God and choosing our own disastrous human nature. We fall apart and think we have a right to our miserable feelings; after all, just look at what happened to us. Disaster, disease, death, doubt, shame, fear—they will rail at us, but we are one of God's greatest assets. We are His asset no matter what else we may have believed in our little warehouse of misbeliefs.

When I was going through a rough period in my life, I came to realize some harsh facts that actually made me feel better. I typed them out and saved them under "Words of Encouragement for the Weary Soul":

In the course of your life:

You're going to be misunderstood.

You're going to be rejected.

You're going to be betrayed.

You're going to be underpaid, undervalued, and unappreciated.

You're going to be abused, laughed at, put down, and ignored.

You'll lose things, relationships, money, and time.

Get over yourself.

How often our efforts are misunderstood. How often we go unrecognized, unnoticed for heroic deeds. I'll tell you what. It's about time we shrug our shoulders, take a deep breath, and get over ourselves. (These may not be words you'd expect to hear from your therapist, but if I can follow my own advice, I'll offer it to you too.)

I've been privileged to write several biographies of outstanding Christians, and one of the most life-changing, earth-shaking experiences for me was writing *The Emancipation of Robert Sadler*. At the time, I was a published poet, but I had never written a biography. I was very young and very conscientious. It took me a year to write the book. I traveled with Sadler (with my two children); I interviewed dozens of people; I photographed, recorded, researched, and wrote, working hard to get his story down with accuracy and clarity. This black man in his sixties was a former slave, sold by his father for beer money when he was only six years old to a plantation owner along with his two sisters. The remarkable thing about this great man of God was his overwhelming love for absolutely everyone. After living through unspeakable cruelty and shame, he had absolutely no bitterness or guile. He's in heaven now, but people who knew him still rave about the love he radiated.

Sadler's life was a living example of Nehemiah 8:10: "The joy of the LORD is your strength." He had given his heart to the Lord in a prayer meeting as a slave, and in later years as a free man, he opened up a mission to help down-and-outers, ministering love and joy that transformed countless lives. His one and only requirement for happiness was maintaining an intimate relationship with the Lord.

Though as a child he never knew real love, Sadler didn't let that keep him from the love of God. He never stopped to wonder if people liked him or not. He was far too consumed with giving love. He was happy. I can't help long for more of us to be like him, so full of God that we exude happiness. He didn't wait to be happy or look for reasons to be happy. He simply was happy, inside and out. He said to me one day, "Marie, we don't need no qualifications to know the joy of the Lord except the Lord Himself."

There Are No Prerequisites for Happiness

There are many restrictions we place on ourselves every day to keep us from going inside to find the happy lives we crave. We worry. We compete. We compare. We lie.

When will you qualify for happiness?

- When you lose weight? Or while you work at losing weight?
- When you win the lottery and generously give 20 percent of your millions to the church?
- When your friends and family tell you you're just fine the way you are?

- When you work hard, making disciplined decisions to bless your life?
- When you decide to be grateful for the material God gave you to work with?

The causes of unhappiness are found in the three excessive *As*. (Note the word *excessive*.)

1. Excessive need for approval. This need causes you to be super-sensitive to anything less than total acceptance and approval.
2. Excessive need for attention. Your yearning for attention becomes compulsive when you work constantly doing good things to get attention, appreciation, and credit—and can't get what you crave.
3. Excessive need for appreciation. If others don't show you appreciation for your hardworking and loving efforts, you're left feeling bereft and rejected.

All three of these needs by themselves are healthy and realistic. The danger point is in excessiveness.

Examine your expectations and your demands that things go the way you want them to go. Pause and release your fears and concerns of the moment and think about some of the smallest things in your world as comforting and sweet. I'm reminded of some lines the poet gives us in *Leaves of Grass* where he writes about a leaf of grass as no less important than the journey of the stars or the narrowest hinge in his hand.[5]

When's the last time you thanked God for the hinges of your hand? Can you celebrate a leaf of grass? Do you thank God for the stars' journey across the galaxy? Try writing a poem of gratitude in your happiness journal today.

I believe the Lord is encouraging your heart at this moment and telling you you're going to do just fine. He's telling you you're going to prosper, you're going to reach your goals. I know this because that's what His Word says. Think of yourself as favored. In the book of Leviticus, He explains His favor to His chosen ones (which includes you): "For I will look on you favorably and make you fruitful, multiply you and confirm My covenant with you" (26:9). His favor lasts. It doesn't come and go depending on His mood. "His favor is for life" (Ps. 30:5).

Reality is that we live in an unhappy world. But I'm ringing the wake-up bell to snap you out of a quasi-religious panic so you can recognize it's *you* who makes you unhappy and not the unhappy world you live in.

The apostle Paul tells us in the book of Romans that the sufferings of this present time aren't worthy to be compared with the glory that awaits us (8:18). It's the "flesh" that sneaks up on us. The Greek word translated as "flesh" is *sarx*, and Paul tells us to "make no provision for the *sarx*" (13:14).

Living in the *sarx* means making decisions and performing actions apart from faith and God's indwelling Spirit. *Sarx* is displeasing to the Lord. It's what's in us that hasn't been transformed by God. We aren't to feed our self-centered human nature. We're to feed our spirits with the power of the Holy Spirit in order to be conquerors of the defeating, negative grip of a hostile devil and a hostile, unhappy world.

Vera Wang, the famous fashion designer, spent her youth as a figure skater. She got up at four in the morning, skated before school, and after school went back to the rink and skated until eight o'clock at night. Three days a week she took ballet lessons for an hour and a half. Summers she went to skating camp, and by noon she already had skated seven hours. She competed for fifteen years and won many regional championships. She was among the top singles skaters in the United States for almost five years. She says daily discipline "was ingrained into me in a way that, at sixty, I still possess [it] and [it] will still be with me every single day of my life." She goes on to say, "Were it not for what I learned through skating, I could never have reached my dream of becoming a designer. Those principles of discipline, desire, and hard work are one hundred percent responsible for my success."[6]

Your success at living a fulfilled and gratified inner life depends on how much effort you put into your spiritual training. Happiness is a skill that with God's grace you teach yourself. Your natural ability to be happy will only take you so far.

Just as a champion runner, skater, or gymnast practices daily, you too need to practice daily your happiness skills; you must practice the deep inner work that takes all your effort and your entire mind. For the rest of your life, you're in training.

What Will You Do with Today?

Steve Jobs, the cofounder of Apple, was adopted as an infant. He was teased that his parents didn't want him. Nothing deterred his creativity as he grew up, and when he was in his early fifties, he said, "For the past thirty-three years I have looked in the mirror every morning and asked myself, 'If today were the last day of my life, would I want to do what I am about to do today?' And whenever the answer has been 'no,' for too many days in a row, I know I need to change something."[7]

If this were the last day of your life, would you want to do what you're about to do?

Do what you are afraid to do.

Give where you are afraid to give.

Ask what you are afraid to ask.

See what you are afraid to see.

Negativity may be around you, but it doesn't have to be *in* you.

Let go of your pride, your love of doing things your way, and your love of worldly influences. Don't wait until you're old to see how beautiful you are.

You're like a starfish, one of the most amazing of God's creations. If a starfish loses one of its arms, it can actually regenerate and grow a new one. You're made like that too. God is in the restoration business. You can regenerate the inner parts of yourself you've lost. There have been times in my life when I've lost joy. I've lost faith in men. I've lost a sense of self-worth. But my broken, frozen heart has been regenerated.

These words of the apostle Paul have yanked me out of the doubt and self-pity pits more than once: "Who shall separate us from the love of Christ? Shall tribulation, or distress, or persecution, or famine, or nakedness, or peril, or sword? . . . In all these things we are more than conquerors through Him who loved us" (Rom. 8:35, 37).

And then the kicker:

> I am persuaded that neither death nor life, nor angels nor principalities nor powers, nor things present nor things to come, nor height nor depth, nor any other created thing, shall be able to separate us from the love of God which is in Christ Jesus our Lord. (Rom. 8:38–39)

Forgive the world and its unfairness. Stop asking why bad things happen to good people. Here's a list of twelve lasting happiness gifts to give to yourself. If you follow these twelve points, you'll discover the freedom and happiness you deserve and long for. Copy them into your happiness journal.

1. Today I will be happy. I will be happy with myself, my work, and my endeavors. I will be happy with what I have and where I am.
2. Today I will not try to change the world to fit my demands and expectations. I will be at peace with the world and the people around me.
3. Today I will bless my body by exercising, eating nutritiously, and declining the temptation to neglect my health.
4. Today I will discover something new and interesting. I will do this by studying, reading, observing, or listening. I will record on paper at least one new thing that I discover today.

5. Today I will do something good for someone else. I'll try to do it so they don't know I was the one who did it. I will be a channel of blessing for someone today because I am a giver.

6. Today I will look as good as I can and be glad about it. I will dress thoughtfully and carry myself with dignity.

7. Today I will not find fault or criticize one person, and I will not try to change anyone against their will.

8. Today I will live this day only and not try to conquer all of life at once.

9. Today I will make a plan for myself. I will schedule my hours and not allow my enemies, rush and indecision, to overwhelm my precious time.

10. Today I will give myself the right to make mistakes, to be imperfect, and still feel good. Today I will not be led by misbeliefs. Today I will believe I am worthy of being loved.

11. Today I won't put two things in the same area of space. I won't put doubt and faith in the same heart.

12. Today I will be an example to everyone I meet. I can be happy in an unhappy world.

As I write the last paragraph of this book, I sense more of a fantastic beginning than a conclusion. I'll always be a pilgrim on the happiness journey, and in writing this book, I've shared moments in the lives of other pilgrims, and a part of me is in each of their stories. I relate to every person who pays the price to pull themselves out of the hungry jaws of an unhappy world and an unhappy self. I've written this book as evidence that it's possible to be happy in an unhappy world and to know happiness in a lasting way. I pray you'll increase your Quiet Prayer life and go forward as the treasure you are in a world that needs every bit of happiness you can bring it. You and I know the best things in life aren't things. Happiness is everything. Please come back and visit these pages again and again.

Love,
Marie

Notes

Introduction

1. William Backus and Marie Chapian, *Telling Yourself the Truth* (Minneapolis: Bethany House, 2000), 17–18.

2. Steven Pressfield, *The War of Art* (New York: Black Irish Entertainment, 2012), 40.

Chapter 1: Good-bye to the Victim

1. Viktor Frankl, *Man's Search for Meaning* (Cutchoque, NY: Buccaneer Books, 1993), 75.

2. Erich Fromm, *The Art of Loving* (New York: Harper & Row, 1956), 19.

3. St. Catherine of Genoa, *Life and Doctrine of Saint Catherine of Genoa*, ed. Paul A. Boer Sr. (New York: Christian Press Assoc. Publishing Company, 1907).

Chapter 2: The Call to Happiness

1. Arthur Schopenhauer, *On the Suffering of the World* (New York: Penguin, 2004), 5.

2. Ludwig Wittgenstein, Ludwig Wittgenstein Quotes, Goodreads.com, accessed June 16, 2015, http://www.goodreads.com/author/quotes/7672.Ludwig _Wittgenstein.

Chapter 3: The Perfectionist

1. Bronnie Ware, *The Top Five Regrets of the Dying* (Carlsbad, CA: Hay House, 2012), v.

Chapter 5: The Magnitude of Loss

1. Leonard Berkowitz, *Aggression: Its Causes, Consequences, and Control* (Philadelphia: Temple University Press, 1994).

Chapter 6: The Search for Success in an Unhappy World

1. Cambridge Dictionaries Online, s.v. "success," http://dictionary.cambridge
.org/us/dictionary/american-english/success.
2. Gavriel Zaloshinsky, ed., *The Ways of the Tzaddikim* (Nanuet, NY: Feld-
heim Publishers, 1995).
3. Guilaume Apollinaire, Guilaume Apollinaire Quotes, BrainyQuote.com,
accessed June 16, 2015, http://www.brainyquote.com/quotes/authors/g/guillaume
_apollinaire.html.
4. Missy Franklin, quoted in Chad Bonham, "A Conversation with U.S. Olym-
pian Missy Franklin," Beliefnet.com, accessed June 16, 2015, http://www.belief
net.com/columnists/inspiringathletes/2012/06/a-conversation-with-u-s-olympian
-missy-franklin.html.
5. Steve Jobs, "'You've Got to Find What You Love,' Jobs Says," *Stanford News*,
June 14, 2005, http://news.stanford.edu/news/2005/june15/jobs-061505.html.
6. Phil Mahre, "1-2 and Baby Makes 3," *New York Times*, February 20, 1984,
http://www.nytimes.com/1984/02/20/sports/1-2-and-baby-makes-3.html.
7. Edmund Bergler, *Selected Papers, 1933–1961* (New York: Grune & Strat-
ton, 1969).

Chapter 7: Work and Happiness

1. George Lehner and Ella Kube, *The Dynamics of Personal Adjustment* (New
York: Prentice Hall, 1955).
2. Mother Teresa, *No Greater Love* (Novato, CA: The World Library, 2001).

Chapter 9: The Fears That Kill You

1. Henri Nouwen, *Bread for the Journey* (New York: HarperOne, 2006), 26.
2. John of the Cross, *Selected Writings*, ed. Kieran Kavanaugh (New York:
Paulist Press, 1987), 271.
3. Saint Faustina, *Diary: Divine Mercy in My Soul*, 3rd ed. (Stockbridge, MA:
Marian Press, 2005).
4. Maria Etter Woodworth, *Signs and Wonders* (New Kensington, PA: Whita-
ker House, 1997).
5. Joan of Arc, Joan of Arc Quotes, BrainyQuote.com, accessed June 16, 2015,
http://www.brainyquote.com/quotes/authors/j/joan_of_arc.html.
6. Charles S. Carver and Ronald J. Ganellen, "Depression and Components
of Self-Punitiveness," *Journal of Abnormal Psychology* 92, no. 3 (1983): 330–37.
7. Lois Joy Hofmann, *Maiden Voyage: In Search of Adventure and Moments
of Bliss* (San Diego: PIP Productions, 2010).

Chapter 10: Beloved

1. Marie Chapian, *Talk to Me, Jesus: Journal and Devotional* (Racine, WI:
Broadstreet Publishers, 2015).
2. Mickey O'Neill McGrath, OSFS, www.bromickeymcgrath.com.

3. Julian of Norwich, *Revelations of Divine Love*, ed. Dom Roger Hudleston, OSB (Mineola, NY: Dover, 2006), 7.

4. John Ramsey, with Marie Chapian, *The Other Side of Suffering* (New York: Faith Words, Hachette Book Group, 2012).

Chapter 11: The Loveaholic

1. Fromm, *Art of Loving*, 19.

2. James Thurber, *The Thurber Carnival* (New York: Harper Collins, 1999).

Chapter 12: Heart and Soul Happiness

1. Viktor Frankl, Viktor E. Frankl Quotes, Goodreads.com, accessed June 16, 2015, http://www.goodreads.com/author/quotes/2782.Viktor_E_Frankl.

Chapter 13: Your Happy Brain

1. Rick Hanson, "Taking in the Good," RickHanson.net, May 1, 2014, http://www.rickhanson.net/event/taking-good.

2. Chapian, *Talk to Me, Jesus: Journal and Devotional*.

3. Steven Furtick, *Sun Stand Still* (Colorado Springs: WaterBrook Multnomah, 2010), 9.

4. Candace Pert, "Where Do You Store Your Emotions?" CandacePert.com, accessed June 16, 2015, http://candacepert.com/where-do-you-store-your emotions.

5. Norman Doidge, *The Brain That Changes Itself* (New York: Penguin, 2007), 86.

6. Michael Merzenich, quoted in ibid.

Chapter 14: Rest and Idleness for a Happier You

1. Tim Kreider, "The 'Busy' Trap," *New York Times*, June 30, 2012, http://opinionator.blogs.nytimes.com/2012/06/30/the-busy-trap/?_r=0.

2. Thomas Aquinas, Thomas Aquinas Quotes, BrainyQuote.com, accessed June 16, 2015, http://www.brainyquote.com/quotes/quotes/t/thomasaqui186905.html.

3. John Violanti, *Dying for the Job: Police Work Exposure and Health* (Springfield, IL: Charles C. Thomas Publishing, 2014), 79.

4. Rebecca Smith-Coggins, "Improving Alertness and Performance in Emergency Department Physicians and Nurses: The Use of Planned Naps," *Annals of Emergency Medicine* 48, no. 5 (2006): 596–604.

5. Amber Brooks and Leon Lack, "A Brief Afternoon Nap Following Nocturnal Sleep Restriction: Which Nap Duration Is Most Recuperative?" *Sleep* 29, no. 6 (2006): http://journalsleep.org/ViewAbstract.aspx?pid=26564.

6. M. G. Berman, J. Jonides, and S. Kaplan, "The Cognitive Benefits of Interacting with Nature," *Psychological Science* 19, no. 12 (2008): 1207–12.

7. Ovid, Ovid Quotes, BrainyQuote.com, http://www.brainyquote.com/quotes/quotes/o/ovid159352.html.

8. Henri Nouwen, *The Way of the Heart* (New York: Ballantine Books, 1981), 16.

9. Thomas Merton, *A Merton Reader*, ed. Thomas P. McDonnell (New York: Image Books, 1989), 476.

10. John O'Donohue, *Eternal Echoes: Exploring Our Yearning to Belong* (New York: Cliff Street Books, 1999).

11. Chapian, *Talk to Me, Jesus: Journal and Devotional*.

Chapter 15: The Beautiful Now

1. Anthony De Mello, *Awareness* (Grand Rapids: Zondervan, 1990), 5.

2. Mike Bickle, *Song of Songs: The Ravished Heart of God Part 1* (Kansas City, MO: Friends of the Bridegroom, 1999).

3. This section was inspired in part by the foreword of Joan Chittister, *Sick, and You Cared for Me: Homilies and Reflections for Cycle B*, ed. Deacon Jim Knipper (Princeton: Clear Faith Publishing, 2012).

Chapter 16: The Happiness Recovery Plan

1. Sidonie-Gabriella Colette, Colette Quotes, Goodreads.com, accessed June 16, 2015, http://www.goodreads.com/author/quotes/51575.Colette.

2. W. Beran Wolfe, *How to Be Happy Though Human* (New York: Farrar & Rinehart, 1931).

3. Saint Faustina, *Diary*.

4. William Faulkner, William Faulkner Quotes, Goodreads.com, accessed June 16, 2015, http://www.goodreads.com/quotes/129450-given-the-choice-between -the-experience-of-pain-and-nothing.

5. Walt Whitman, "Song of Myself," *Leaves of Grass*, www.Bartleby.com /142/14.html.

6. Vera Wang, quoted in Venus Williams, *Come to Win* (New York: Harper-Collins: 2010), 80–82.

7. Steve Jobs, quoted in Jennifer Valentino-DeVries, "Steve Jobs's Best Quotes," Digits, October 5, 2012, http://blogs.wsj.com/digits/2012/10/05/steve-jobss-best -quotes-2/.

Additional Sources

Bourgeault, Cynthia. *Centering Prayer and Inner Awakening.* Lanham, MD: Cowley Publications, 2004.

Chapian, Marie, with Robert Sadler. *The Emancipation of Robert Sadler.* Minneapolis: Bethany House, 2012.

Coyle, Neva, and Marie Chapian. *The All-New Free to Be Thin.* Minneapolis: Bethany House, 1993.

Nettle, Daniel. *Happiness: The Science behind Your Smile.* Oxford, NY: Oxford University Press, 2005.

Tamir, Diana I., and Jason P. Mitchell. *Disclosing Information about the Self Is Intrinsically Rewarding.* Cambridge: Harvard University Press, Proceedings of the National Academy of Sciences, 2012.

Acknowledgments

I need to thank many people, such as my mentor and friend Dr. William Backus, who, along with his wife, Candy, showed me I was a truly worthwhile person at a time when I felt abandoned and alone. Bill encouraged me to become a professional therapist and convinced me I could actually start at the bottom of the ladder and not fall off. Bill is now in heaven, and I will always be grateful for his encouragement and support as I labored through my years of schooling and clinical internship. I was privileged to write two books with him, *Telling Yourself the Truth* and *Why Do I Do What I Don't Want to Do?*

Many thanks to Christa Chapian, whose help with the preparation of this manuscript was invaluable; Mario Lombardo for reading the first drafts; my prayer partners and co-workers at Wings of Wellness for help and support as I wrote; my international HIM family for prayers; my terrific agents at ALIVE, Joel Kneedler and Lisa Jackson; and my wonderful editors, Lonnie Hull DuPont and Jessica English.

I would be remiss if I didn't thank my students, patients, and clients who've reached the top of your mountains and who continue to teach me much as I'm privileged to walk alongside you on your happiness journeys. I'm forever proud of you for pressing on, never giving up, and always aiming for the best of God. I also thank all the people who willingly took part in my happiness surveys. I love each of you for your honesty and your willingness to learn and grow beyond the status quo. I humbly and wholly thank you all. You have made this project a happy one and, most of all, confirmed that lasting happiness is not an elusive pie-in-the-sky endeavor, but a living reality we can teach ourselves to experience and keep.

Marie Chapian is a *New York Times* bestselling author of over thirty books, including the popular *Telling Yourself the Truth* with William Backus. She is a counselor, seminar leader, certified life and fitness coach, and director of Wings of Wellness. She lives in Southern California.

For more information about Marie Chapian's How to Be Happy in an Unhappy World workshops and seminars, Quiet Prayer materials, body-soul-spirit classes, videos, and online courses, visit www.mariechapian.com.

You can recover from depression or avoid it altogether.

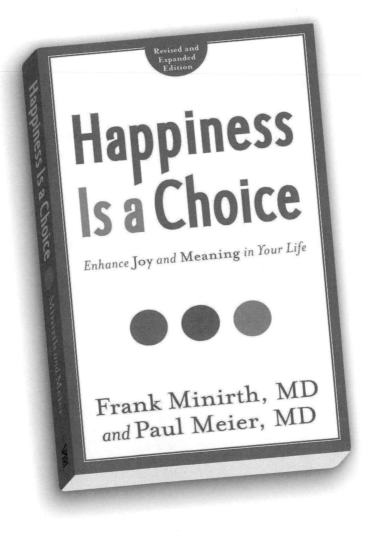

Drs. Minirth and Meier will show you the steps to a happy and fulfilling life.

From bestselling author
KAY WARREN

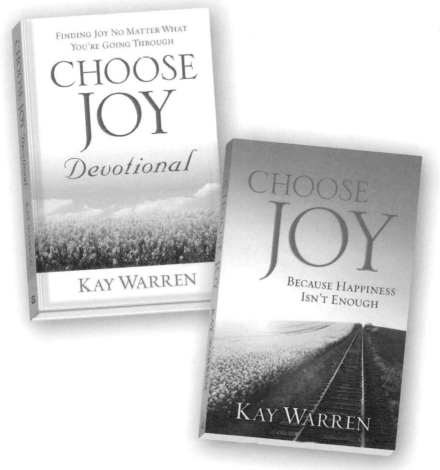

In *Choose Joy*, acclaimed author and Christian leader Kay Warren explains the path to experiencing soul-satisfying joy no matter what you're going through. Joy is deeper than happiness, lasts longer than excitement, and is more satisfying than pleasure and thrills. Joy is richer. Fuller. And it's far more accessible than you've thought.

Bestsellers That Continue to Change Lives and Relationships

You can be positive—no matter who tries to bring you down. Unfortunately, the world is full of screwed-up people. But the good news is your world no longer has to revolve around them. You can stop being the victim of others and start loving life in spite of them.